Also by Betsy & Warren Talbot

Books

Married with Luggage: What We Learned About Love by Traveling the World

Dream Save Do: An Action Plan for Dreamers

Strip Off Your Fear: The Good Girl's Guide to Saying What You Want

In Confidence: Essays in Bold Living

Course

Declutter Clinic - a self-paced, step-by-step course to help you remove the clutter from your life and home

Learn more about these books and the authors' journey from the brink of divorce to traveling the world together
at
www.MarriedwithLuggage.com

Dream Save Do

An Action Plan for Dreamers Like You

Betsy and Warren Talbot

Dedicated to Betsy's brother Bo Gray and our close friend Maria Ross, who inspired us to take action on our dreams. We cannot imagine our lives without you in them.

Contents

A Note from the Authors

We blame the President of Ecuador. How could he allow a political coup attempt – complete with rioting police, burning tires in the street, and soap opera style dramatics – to happen on the day we planned to arrive at the first stop on our long-awaited trip around the world?

We couldn't believe our luck. We had just spent the last 2 years transitioning from middle-aged yuppies to backpacking world travelers. We had quit our jobs, sold our house, and gotten rid of everything we owned except what was carefully packed in our backpacks. Our bank account was filled with the money we aggressively saved and earned.

We were suited up in our travel clothes and ready to go, and we could only sit slack-jawed as we watched the international news reports. The airport in Quito, Ecuador was shut down as the military took control, and the borders with Peru and Colombia were closed. Travel on the Pan American Highway, the main artery through all of South America, was blockaded in Ecuador.

Over the course of the previous 2 years we learned how to prioritize life over money, experience over possessions, and relationships over status. Political unrest was the one thing we didn't learn how to handle. Fortunately our big life upheaval did prepare us for venturing into the unknown, so we kept moving forward.

"We have political drama every few years; it'll blow over soon." This was the feedback from our Colombian friend in Seattle, and she backed it up by giving us the names and phone numbers of her relatives in Colombia and Ecuador just in case. While I'm sure this was meant to reassure us, it did the exact opposite.

We got on the plane and decided to at least get to our first stop in Miami. We met up with friends and spent our layover eating Cuban food and sipping mojitos on the beach. We still didn't know what country we'd be sleeping in the next night, but it gradually became more of a curiosity than a worry. After all, didn't we remake our lives so we could have more adventure? The more we starting leaning into the situation, the better we felt about the outcome.

When we made it back to the airport we discovered the Quito airport was reopened, but the news replay of the president getting tear-gassed by his own police force did little to encourage optimism. Again, we depended on the skills we learned over 2 years of planning for this trip, making difficult choices and weighing the benefits on an almost daily basis, and we worked out a plan. We'd go to Quito (this is a country heavily dependent on tourism, after all, so it was in their best economic interest to get back to normal ASAP). If it looked dangerous when we got there, we'd book a short flight over to Bogota without ever leaving the airport.

We sat next to a midlevel Ecuadorian government official on the flight in, and he told us not to worry. He then went on to highlight some of the exotic places we should see, the foods we should try, and the events we should experience. He, like our Colombian friend in Seattle, made it seem like the news was just a soap opera set to entertain and real life was far more serene. We're happy to say, he was right.

When we arrived at the airport we did find armed guards, but it was the normal situation for the airport and the workers showed the same bored disdain they do all over the world. We were lazily stamped into the country and shuffled out to our cab just like we've done dozens of times before and since.

Ecuador became our home for the next 3 months as we learned Spanish, made new friends, and experienced a diverse and beautiful country. Had we given in to our initial worries at the first report of danger, we would likely not be living the life we are now, traveling the world and living our dream.

This is a more exotic example of the type of roadblocks stopping people every single day from living their dream. At the first sign of difficulty, most people back down, assessing the effort as too great. In reality, the biggest effort is usually a mental one. Get over that, take the first step, and the rest happens in fairly logical fashion. This has been proven over and over again in our lives.

As we've continued traveling the world since then, we can't believe we ever doubted our ability to do it. The work was worth it a thousand times over, and the life we have today – living in exotic places, meeting fascinating people, and absorbing new cultures – is one we cannot imagine ever giving up.

We've learned how to navigate an attempted coup, survive an erupting volcano, withstand a Force-12 storm in Antarctica's Drake Passage, and enjoy a large family reunion in Mongolia's Gobi Desert without speaking the language. We've also learned the more challenging skills of saying what we really want, standing up to peer pressure, and trusting in ourselves to figure things out when we don't have all the answers. Whether your dream involves travel or not, these are the skills that will take you wherever you want to go.

*When you learn to achieve your dreams,
nothing seems impossible anymore.*

It's all a matter of figuring out the logistics and taking action, one of the most valuable life lessons you'll ever learn.

We wrote this book for other dreamers, people with unrealistic visions of what life could be. Do you:

- Imagine waking up every day to a life you love, doing meaningful work, enjoying relationships with great people, pursuing your hobbies and interests in your free time, and living exactly how and where you've always wanted?
- Think about how it would feel to know you made your own lifestyle dream come true and how much confidence it would give you in attaining other things in your life?
- Envision the kind of people you would meet and know if you were living the way you really wanted to? You'd be having dinner together, going on trips, calling each other for advice, and helping each other out. You'd actually *be* one of the people you respect now.

Your dream lifestyle is not out of reach. It is the life we live every single day, and we're not so different from you.

Our lives before were uninspiring, but from the outside looking in we had nothing to complain about. We had good jobs, a decent place to live, and enough money to eat out and go on vacation every year. We weren't unhappy, but we were far from fulfilled. There was something missing, and we kept looking to our jobs and money to find it.

Maybe you feel the same way, a little bit adrift and somewhat guilty for not being happy with what you already have. All your basic needs are covered, but there's a hole, and you may or may not be clear on how to fill it.

The Inspiration for Change

When my brother had a heart attack at age 35, we finally got the clarity we'd been missing: Life is short. We stopped looking for fulfillment in fleeting things like money and status and decided to chase our biggest desires: freedom and experience. This book is the roadmap we used to create the lifestyle of our dreams.

Our missing piece happened to be simplicity and travel, but even if yours is completely different – like starting a business, running a marathon, or building a house – this book will show you how to visualize it, put a price tag on it, accumulate the cash, change your habits, and rally your friends and family to make it a reality. Even if you just have a fuzzy idea of what you want to do, we can help.

This is an Action Plan for Dreamers, full of practical advice and real-life examples to help you create the reality you want in your life. This plan has been tested out by hundreds of dreamers just like you. It works whether your dream is to open a business, write your first book, or travel the world. We've done every single thing in this book, and plenty of other people have road-tested our wisdom since.

We published the first edition of this book in 2011, and we weren't prepared for the response. People were *hungry* for the recipe of the life we created and wanted to know how to duplicate it. They discovered we were all about practical steps and visible results and wanted more of our no-BS straight talk to coach them through their dreams.

Over the following months, people began emailing to tell us how they made the plan work for them.

- A single mother set a goal to grow her side business into a full-time gig and dump her dead-end day job so she could spend more time with her son. She sent us a thank-you note one day before her self-imposed deadline to tell us she had done it – and received a lucrative book deal in the process.

- A father wrote to us about his family's failed attempt at an international sabbatical the year before and how our plan showed him the flaw in his earlier system. After revising their strategy, his family was able to make the 3-month trip to Indonesia a reality and start a bakery wholesale business to boot.

- A professional woman was inspired by our story to turn a job layoff into the jumpstart for a dream of teaching internationally. She used our plan to focus on how it could work instead of why it wouldn't and now lives and teaches in Brazil.

- A recent PhD graduate with bipolar disorder took our book and learned how to design work around her life. Instead of taking the structured job waiting for her (which she knew would aggravate her condition) she created an entirely virtual career of writing and consulting with very few physical possessions. She is far more satisfied every day, and when the need for change arises she can easily pick up her laptop and go without disrupting her career.

- A busy mom told us she always wanted to bake fancy cakes, but after a move to a rural place for her husband's job and a tight income, she wasn't sure how she'd ever start the business. She took our advice on how to put a price tag on her dream and found it was cheaper to start a cake business than she thought, and her long-held dream became a successful reality within a few short months.

This Action Plan for Dreamers works. People have been using it to create and fund their own dream lifestyles since 2011, and we regularly get emails from people achieving their biggest goals.

Our greatest satisfaction comes from the readers who weren't exactly sure what their dream might be until they started focusing on their lives to figure it out. They've gone from treading water to actually swimming.

We are firm believers in a series of small, everyday steps in making great life change. This book is our Action Plan for Dreamers of all ages and types.

This is in part a personal finance book. You'll learn to use money as a tool to reach your goals instead of a goal in and of itself.

This is also a relationship book where you will learn through daily action how to improve your existing relationships with friends, family, your mate, and even yourself as you create the life of your dreams. In addition, you'll learn how to meet new people who want the same things you do.

This is a happiness book, because by the sheer nature of working every day to make your life fit around your interests, you'll become happier and more satisfied with the life you have.

This is an Action Plan for Dreamers, taking your deepest desires and bringing them to life through focused and everyday action.

No doubt about it, this is an intense process. You will be overwhelmed at the speed with which your dream starts coming together when you take action, and we want you to be prepared for it.

This is the plan of how we did it, and it is a plan for you to do it, too. Your dream is right around the corner, and you just took the first step.

Now let's get to it.

– February 5, 2013

Guanajuato, Mexico

Introduction

"You're so lucky!"
"I wish I could do that!"
"Must be nice!"

These are the phrases we often hear when we tell people we are traveling around the world, and they are all true. How did we get so lucky to live this life?

People want to know our secret, the magic recipe, the special power that helped us go from corporate workers to world travelers. They want to know a quick answer to help them accomplish their own specific dreams and we have one:

Spend less than you earn.
Save what's left.

It's not a revolutionary answer, but you can better understand the power of it when you see the 2012 household saving rate across the English-speaking world (that's how much you save of the "extra" money you have left after paying your bills). It is a mere 3.7% in the US, 3.5% in Canada, 5.3% in the UK, 2.9% in New Zealand and a whopping 8.9% in Australia. This means if you have $100 left, you are saving less than the amount of coins you probably have jingling in your pocket right now.

It's no wonder more people aren't living their dreams. It's hard to do it when spare change is all you've got to spare for your life's biggest ambition.

But change doesn't come easy, even when faced with proof life will be better. It's why people still smoke, stay in unhealthy relationships, eat poorly, and sink further into debt. The devil you know is more comforting than the one you don't.

Researchers have studied the resistance to change for years, and the transtheoretical model (TTM) was developed to explain it. In essence, there are 5 stages of change:

- Pre-contemplation: There is no conscious intention to make a change. It often takes an outside influence to move you to the next stage. "Things will never change, so why try?"
- Contemplation: You realize the behavior is a problem, but you're still ambivalent to take action. "I know I'd be happier in a new relationship, but it's too much work to get out of this one."
- Preparation: You know you must change and have begun preparing to do so. You buy this book, sign up for a class, buy a nicotine patch, or write your "Dear John" letter.
- Action: You're doing what you said you would do and feeling the benefits and challenges of a new lifestyle. "I am saving money every month and can see my dream taking shape."
- Maintenance: After 6 months, your new behavior is in maintenance mode. This is where you work to cement it into your life long-term. "I don't charge more on my credit card than I can pay off at the end of the

month. I like my financial freedom too much."

According to this scale, you are now at the Preparation stage on the continuum of change. How does that make you feel? You aren't starting at the beginning; you're midway through and ready to get serious about reaching the finish line.

This is where our Action Plan for Dreamers comes in. You'll get more than a stern lecture to "spend less than you earn" because you already know this. You'll learn how to come up with a compelling reason to change your life (or else why would you?), how to make it a reality, how to recover when you stumble (because you will), and how to adjust to your life as it morphs into your dream (not always a smooth ride!). You'll get step-by-step instructions on amassing serious cash with advice for challenges and pitfalls along the way.

We'll show you how to:

- Automate your savings to bypass willpower issues (hey, why test it if you don't have to?)
- Create some homemade porn (but not the kind you think!) to keep you motivated
- Build your first crappy budget and then make it into a great one
- Combat peer pressure
- Recover from the inevitable slip-ups along the way
- Live large on a small entertainment budget

This Action Plan for Dreamers is going to show you how to stockpile loads of money in a relatively short period of time so you can create something new in your life. It's also going to show you how to transition your life in stages to the one you've always wanted. You will never,

ever look at your life the same way again – and that's a very good thing.

We have a pretty good idea where you are right now because we had those same feelings of just not knowing what to do. We wanted to change our lives but we didn't know how. It wasn't until two people very close to us came down with life-threatening illnesses that we finally forced ourselves into action, and that's when we learned the biggest secret of all.

> *Scheming and dreaming will only fill your mind. Taking action will fill your life.*

It doesn't matter that you don't know how something will turn out or exactly how you're going to do it. It doesn't matter that you don't know all the answers (who does, by the way?). What matters is that you take the first step immediately and continue taking action every day until you reach your dream.

We learned this lesson as we saved and worked toward our dream of world travel, realizing that all those questions we had at the start were magically answered along the way because we were forcing them to be addressed. Now you're going to learn to do the same thing.

The guide is set up in 3 sections:

Dream: Crystallize your dream and know what a day in the life looks like so you can figure out what it will actually cost. Not quite sure of your dream yet? We've got that covered, too. (If you already know exactly what you desire, you can skip to Chapter 2.) We'll show you how to create the kind of lifestyle to invite dreams in, maintain your motivation, and set the date.

Save: Save, sell, find: We'll show you all the ways you can amass the cash – more quickly than you thought – to finance your dream. You'll also find out some creative ways to save while maintaining some of your comforts and have fun along the way.

Do: Action is the name of the game in this section. You'll learn how to earn extra money, evaluate your saving and spending every month, and what to do when you screw up. You'll find out how to rally your friends and family to your cause and what to do if some of them are working against you. You'll learn how to combat peer pressure and create a lifestyle of dream achievement.

Throughout the book you'll read specific scenarios from our story to illustrate the lessons we learned from our experience as well as how we made it through the rough patches unscathed. You'll also get a glimpse into the lives of people who have also successfully used this plan to achieve their biggest dreams.

We'll also reveal the key components to our savings plan:

THE VAULT is the account where you will keep your money. It is a one-way street. You can't touch this. In fact, imagine a big guard dog in front of your Vault door, snarling and barking if you get close (though he will wag his tail and roll on his back for a belly scratch once you reach your goal). Money goes in, but it does not come out until you have hit your goal.

THE ROADMAP is your budget, the guide along this savings journey. You will start out with a crappy one, and your job is to refine it over time, making adjustments every month to move you closer to your goal. We'll show you how to do it, and with automation you'll see how easy it is to make your dream a reality.

DREAM PORN is your big motivation, the reminder you place in a prominent space to keep your goal front and center. This hot stuff will keep you focused on your prize.

PHRASE TO SAVE is the mantra you will develop to keep you on track with your daily spending and celebrate your savings. We'll show you how to develop yours based on your budget numbers and your dream.

At the end of the book, you can view the one-page Action Plan of all the steps for easy reference. Plus you can find downloadable resources under the Tools & Resources section at www.DreamSaveDo.com. You can also read the End Notes for further detail on the research we've used in this book.

One final note: Overall the book's voice is mine (Betsy's) and the pronoun "I" refers to me. The pronoun "we" refers to both Warren and me. We did this to aid with the storytelling and make a co-written book easier to understand. Where we say "you" we obviously mean you. And we'll write to "you" a lot.

We recommend that you read the book through once and then go back and complete the work to take action on your dream. (Though we won't penalize you for jumping right in.)

Now let's begin with putting your money where your mouth is.

Ready to Get Started?

Disclaimer: You know the drill. We can't guarantee you'll have the same level of success as we did, though we can't rule out you achieving more than us, either. We are not financial advisers or attorneys, and we can't be held responsible for anything you do or do not do as a result of this guide.

Your life is yours to design, revise, and improve. *But you already knew that.*

Action Plan for Dreamers

1. Discover Your Dream

2. Make It So Real You Can Touch It

3. Align your Desires with Your Partner

4. Create Dream Porn and Give Your Dream a Name

5. Price Your Dream

6. Set the Date

7. Secure Your Vault

8. Calculate Your Spending

9. Address Credit Card Debt

10. Create Your Phrase to Save

11. Cut Expenses to Make Room for Your Dream

12. Refine Your Roadmap

13. Create Additional Income

14. Perform a Monthly Financial Review

15. Enlist Support and Manage Peer Pressure

16. Enrich More than Your Bank Account

Section I: Dream

or, more accurately, turning your dream into reality

Chapter 1: Discover Your Dream

"There are some people who live in a dream world, and there are some who face reality; and then there are those who turn one into the other."

— Douglas H. Everett

The Mile High Bar & Grill at Terminal B in Denver International Airport is not the most romantic setting for a date. Rumpled business travelers nurse their drinks slowly so they don't have to give up their cherished seats before their flights are called. An overhead speaker crackles every few minutes with an unintelligible announcement. The aroma of exhaustion and fried food hangs in the air.

This is where Warren and I met one weeknight as we were flying in opposite directions across the country. We had each left home from Boston a week before, and it would be a few days more before we would be home together. We considered it lucky that we were able to coordinate our flights to meet for a meal.

It was the least romantic time in our lives.

Warren arrived first and snagged us a table. I clickety-clacked across the terminal with my high heels and trolley bag to meet him, wishing for just five minutes in a pair of slippers to relieve my aching feet.

We ordered our food and began catching up. We talked about clients, projects, coworkers, and hotels. Not only were these things keeping us apart on a regular basis, they were even the topics of our conversation when we were together. We were those annoying sound bite chatterers, talking in biz-speak, abbreviations, and lingo that only another cubicle dweller could understand.

At the end of our dinner we both sat staring numbly at each other. We were so damn tired, and we were tired of being tired all the time.

We gathered our things, gave each other a chaste kiss and a hug, and set off in different directions to catch flights to our next destinations for still more meetings. Anyone looking at us would have considered us coworkers, and through circumstances that is exactly what we were becoming.

We're not marriage counselors, but since we had each been previously married and divorced, we knew the signs of impending doom. We were heading down that path.

This wasn't one of those "he doesn't understand me" or "I have to read her mind" kinds of situations. Even scarier, we both knew exactly what was going on and how far away we were from happiness either individually or as a couple.

A few days later we were both back home again. After awkwardly joking about the need to make a date 2000 miles away, we started the uncomfortable conversation about why this lifestyle just wasn't working. Something had to give, and if we didn't want it to be our marriage we had to do something about it immediately.

This is when we began taking our first steps toward a dream, even though we would not have called it that at the time. That conversation was perhaps the hardest of our relationship because we had to admit we were failing, set aside the idea of blame, and work on a solution.

We asked ourselves the question: "Is this how we want to live?"

The only other option was to wait for the steady decline to turn into a conversation about an exit strategy, an option neither of us wanted.

The dream we are living now – exploring the world – started forming from this very desire to not work so much and have more time together as a couple.

Reconnect with Your Joy

The lesson in that story is simple but powerful. When you become disconnected from the joy that feeds your soul, you become disconnected with life, and you're just going through the motions. Nothing is really bad, but nothing is really great either.

Maybe you have become disconnected from your joy, and right now you're trying to find a way back.

Your joy may lie in decreasing the things you *don't* want to do, and that's a great starting point. Being fed up with something is a great motivator for change, and as you move away from what you don't like about your life you'll see new opportunities open up all around you. We'll cover this in detail next.

No matter what your dream is – fully-fledged idea or fuzzy notion or just the conviction that what you're doing now is not working – you'll need money and resources to get from where you are now to where you want to be. We're going to show you how to get it all.

Fitting your lifestyle to your dream

Let's meet Akiyo, a recent PhD graduate in England. She is a smart woman with a bright future, but instead of feeling excited at the prospect of starting her career, she felt stifled. You see, Akiyo has bipolar disorder and has battled it all her life. Besides her everyday management of the illness, she knows to expect a super-manic phase every 4 years or so. When she goes through this, it turns her life upside down. This craving for stimulation encourages her to ignore everything mundane, including her job, education, relationships, and home. These phases typically last about 3 months, or, as she likes to say, long enough to mess up her life. In fact, she typically just leaves them all and starts over fresh. She says the pain, guilt and shame following these episodes is incredible.

With her PhD in hand, the thought of tying herself down to a lecturer's job terrified her. How could she recover after a manic phase in such a conservative environment? How would she maintain her relationships and her home mortgage?

"My boyfriend and I met when I was going through the last bout of this super-manic phase and he watched me go through an enormous amount of guilt," says Akiyo. "He said 'if there's nothing you can do about going through these changes periodically, why don't you set up your life to suit that?' So if I need to move to a new city every 4 years [I should] make that transition easy: own less stuff, rent a house rather than buy (I had bought a house at the time), find a location-independent career, do stuff every day that keeps me stimulated so that I don't get bored of life (and thus want to leave it again)."

We'll return to Akiyo's story later, but we wanted to bring it up now for those of you who aren't quite sure what you want to do but know your current lifestyle is not working for your overall physical, emotional, or social health.

If You Don't Know Where to Start

Some people are just born knowing what they want to do with their lives. They have never *not* wanted to be an astronaut or a veterinarian or an artist, and they begin working toward this dream at a very early age.

Good for them.

But if you are like most people, you didn't inhale your life's purpose with your first breath of air. You feel as if you're drifting, just waiting for something to happen.

You wonder how some people can be so certain about the life they want and wonder if you'll ever feel that way about yours.

The good news is you can.

Why things get in the way of your happiness

There was a powerful Superbowl commercial a few years ago for job search site Monster.com. Small kids were filmed saying things like,

"When I grow up:

- *I want to file all day."*
- *I want to climb my way up to middle management."*
- *I want sunshine blown up my skirt."*

- *I want to be under-appreciated."*
- *I want to be a yes-man."*

For people not working in an ideal job or living the life they wanted, it was a wake-up call to connect with their earlier dreams. No one wants to be any of those things in the ad, but when you don't know what you do want you have a harder time saying no to the wrong things. How can you know they're wrong if you don't know what's right? Mediocrity drifts in because you have nothing with which to combat it.

Before you know it, this limbo leads to getting sunshine blown up your skirt or working full-time as a yes-man. You get caught up in the status quo, following trends and accepting things as they come to you with minimal complaint. You tolerate things a younger you never thought you would: poor health, debt, unfulfilling work, and unhealthy relationships.

It's not all doom and gloom, of course. People can usually manage to live pretty good lives despite a lack of focus. But if you have the nagging feeling things are not as good as they could be – that you are missing out on something, even if you don't know what that is – today is the day you start to find it.

Our date at the Denver International Airport was the sign we needed to start making some changes in our lives. We didn't know then it would end up with a trip around the world, but it was a very necessary step to clear the path to discovering our dream of world travel.

Speaking of paths, it's hard to see the one in front of you if it's covered up. Next we'll focus on the 2-step Action Plan for clearing the way. This will help you clarify your life down to the essentials so you can see your options more clearly. This is the sweet spot when your dreams have a fighting chance of making themselves

known to you and you have the space and energy to bring
them to life.

Step 1: Chipping Away the Negatives

At a time when most artists planned out their pieces,
Michelangelo worked freehand on a block of marble. He
believed he was divinely inspired and simply revealed
what was already underneath. When the inspiration
struck, he worked into the night with a candle on his hat
for light, and was known to shout, "Speak!" to the stone
as he worked. He was pulling out the perfect image,
chipping away at the excess stone blocking the
masterpiece within.

The things that drain your energy, cause you
distress, or add extra work without extra benefit are the
blocks of stone holding you back from identifying your
dreams and making them real. Like Michelangelo, you
must also chip away what is not ideal. When you shout,
"Speak!" to your life, you have to be prepared to listen, to
pay attention (with a candle on your hat if necessary).

What would you NOT miss in your life if it magically went away tomorrow?

- (Job)
- Commute
- Home maintenance
- Soul-sucking relationships
- Debt
- Poor health
- Fatigue

Job —
Car
Storage Unit —
Jewelry
Watches

Take a piece of paper and list every single thing without
guilt. No one else will see the paper but you, and it

doesn't matter if you have 1 thing on the list or 100. There is no judgment here, just a simple exercise to determine the size of the block containing your masterpiece. You have to give your chisel some direction.

What bothers you about each thing specifically?

Because we are creatures of habit, we have a tendency to replay things in our lives. You may hate your job and your relationships and your duties at home because all make you feel subordinate to other people's needs or like people are not listening to you. The irritant might be cleaning house for your entire family every weekend while they relax, but the root problem is feeling unappreciated and not speaking up about your needs.

An insightful exercise on finding the root cause of your dissatisfaction is called The 5 Whys. You continue to ask yourself why something bothers you (5 or more times) until you get to the real problem, one you may not have even realized in your surface complaint.

"I'm broke."

Why?

"Because I spend too much money."

Why?

"Because I want to treat myself."

Why?

"Because I want to feel special."

Why?

"Because at work and at home I get overlooked a lot."

Why?

"Because I never speak up."

Why?

"Because I'm scared of embarrassing myself."

In this case, the exercise reveals someone is broke because she's buying her confidence – or so she thinks. To bolster her attempts at saving more money, she could also work on speaking up at work and home and see how this affects her desire to overspend.

The reason we advocate getting to the root is to understand what is really draining your energy and causing you distress so you won't repeat it with new activities and relationships going forward. It's like your friend who keeps dating losers. Until he/she figures out why, it will be the same type of mate and the same type of turbulent breakup time after time. You don't understand how she can't see it when it is so clear to everyone else. The hard truth is, however, you have the same problem – a 'dive bar full of losers' in some area of your life. Your dive bar could be unfulfilling work, unhealthy relationships, poor health choices, or careless financial habits. You just have to figure out where it is and why you keep going back there for satisfaction when there is none to be had. (You're not alone; we all have a 'dive bar of losers' in some area of our lives.)

In Akiyo's case, she knew her super-manic phases could undo all the hard work she had done in her education, work, and relationships. Rather than fight against it, she made a list of all the things in her life that worked against her management of the disorder: tying herself down with the purchase of a home, owning too many possessions to easily move, and having a job with too much routine to aggravate her bipolar condition. In short, she needed to craft a life of frequent stimulation and change to stay on an even keel.

don't like job → a lot of stress → pressure to perform

→ I'm nervous I'll disapoint →

I overeat → because I get stressed → because I want to distract myself → because I feel happy → false happiness →

What irritants can you change, reduce or eliminate from your life?

This is where you start chipping away. You have a list in front of you along with the real reason each item is slowly driving you mad.

Now you see your irritants in black and white, and now you can do something about them.

Brainstorm at least 3 ways you can change, reduce or eliminate each irritant/root cause in your life. List one action you can do right now, one that would take time but is realistic, and one that is totally off the wall. Don't think about how others will react or what is realistic. Just brainstorm the options without thought or judgment. You might be surprised at how many realistic options you have in front of you (and how reasonable those first two options look when you get to the third one).

Some things you can do right away, like reducing the irritation of your commute by finding a carpool or listening to soothing music, podcasts or books on tape. Others are first steps toward bigger plans, like halting your credit card spending immediately to stop increasing your debt as you begin work to pay it down, leaving the junk food at the store to begin your path back to health, or rebalancing your relationships as you learn to speak up for yourself.

In the instance of the weekend housework, you may discover you are doing more than expected by your family, or that they think you enjoy housework or that their efforts won't live up to your expectations. A conversation with them about the problem may be all it takes to rebalance the workload, saving you from vacuuming around them with resentment on Saturday afternoon as they surf the Internet and watch movies.

In Akiyo's case, she decided to get rid of the possessions she felt were holding her down. She began by living in just one room of her house. She moved her bed into the living room along with her clothes and books. Whatever didn't fit got sold or donated. She lived like this for a few months before she decided it would work, and then she sold her house to move into a rental with far more long-term flexibility.

She said no to the lecturer's job waiting for her at graduation, and she began looking for location-independent work she could do from her laptop anywhere in the world. She saved a lot of money in anticipation of her new life.

Akiyo's chipping away of the negatives took about a year. As you start chipping away, remember you don't have to change everything at once. Focus on one thing at a time, appreciating the space that opens up when you do and how your overall energy level and outlook changes in response.

Step 2: Adding In the Possibilities

Once you've started chipping away at the negatives, you'll have more space and energy in your life. It's a good feeling, one that will give you better rest at night, more fulfilling relationships, and more energy to pursue the things you enjoy. You won't feel the need to crash out on the couch every evening just to recover from your day. So let's find a place for you to utilize this newfound energy for happiness.

What would you like to add to your life?

Much like you imagined your life without its irritants before, now you are going to imagine the possibilities. This list is sometimes harder than the negatives list because we so easily identify what is not working. Possibilities are often more subtle, and it takes some time to draw them out.

What existing things would you like more of in your life? Exercise, friendship, free time, alone time, parties, travel, writing, culture, cooking, gardening, yoga, meditation, etc.

What new things interest you? Learn a language, fly on a trapeze, dance the tango, make a movie, start a business, etc. For inspiration, check out other people's lists at 43 Things or see what kind of meetups or classes are going on in your area. Write down anything that sparks your interest as a possibility.

How would you like to share your gifts with the world? Volunteer for a cause you support through your time, talents, and connections.

What inspires you about each possibility?

Just like we analyzed the negatives, we're going to find out what energizes you about these possibilities and what needs they fill.

When you know exactly what feeds your soul, you can easily find more of it for your life.

Your interests may all feed into one overall interest, like helping other people, feeding your creativity, discovering new things, or deepening your relationships. You can use The 5 Whys for this exercise, too, getting down to the root of why you really like to do certain types of things more than others. Perhaps you like diverse things like scrapbooking events, your running group, and book club all for the same reason – you get to do these normally 'solo' hobbies with other people. This is the magic, knowing what energizes you and looking for more of it to add to your life.

After downsizing and saving money, Akiyo was ready to start thinking about the possibilities. Because she craved change and new experiences, she and her boyfriend decided to move from England to Edinburgh, Scotland, a place familiar enough to find work but exotic enough to feed their curiosity. They rented a small apartment and she began taking classes in everything from jewelry making to trapeze lessons, and she volunteered in her spare time. She began writing a book. As she indulged her need for stimulation and change, she found herself happier than she had ever been.

Try new experiences on for size

This is where you start adding experiences to your life. Your list gives you a starting point to try things on and see what fits in the newly opened space in your life. Put a check mark next to a few you want to try first.

Some you can 'test drive' almost immediately, like signing up for a class or buying season tickets to your local playhouse. Others you can begin in small ways, like walking around the block after dinner every evening as you work up to more heart pounding exercise.

Your bigger goals will take some time, like learning a complex skill, starting a business, or writing a book, but you can start taking steps now to make them happen. The important thing is to be open to new opportunities and to look for the types of relationships and activities that feed your spirit.

Exercise → feel strong → feel healthy → confident
travel → independent → challenging → stronger person
Start a business → feel accomplished → my own blood sweat tears → feel useful → independent

If you are looking for direction, an effective strategy is to imagine what an ideal day in your life would look like.

- How would you feel when you woke up?
- What would you eat for breakfast?
- How would you spend your day?
- What kind of people would you know?
- Where would you live?

When you have this idea firmly visualized, start thinking of the components that make up this ideal day. For instance, if you imagine yourself hanging out with artists or creative people, you can start by looking for those kinds of friends now at art classes, art school, or even the funky coffee shop filled with local artists' work. If you want to be healthier, you'll have to start exercising and eating better now. If you want to eventually live in a farmhouse, it's time to stop buying things for your city apartment.

Whatever you visualize as your perfect day can begin to take shape with your actions now.

Creating Your Dream Lifestyle

More than likely, you will be stronger at one of these actions than another. I am more of a "strip away the negatives" kinda gal and Warren is more of an "add up the possibilities" kind of guy. But we each employ the two strategies to create the lives we want, and when we can work together toward those goals it is even more powerful.

The beauty of this process is that it works for everyone on every type of goal. It is fully customizable to you. You can create a life with more of what energizes you and less of what drains you.

And that, friend, is the recipe for happily ever after. As you start honing in on your dream lifestyle by streamlining your life to what really works for you, you can follow our plan to start banking the cash you'll need to make it happen.

Chapter Summary

It's okay if you don't know what your big dream is right now. In fact, many people don't. But you can start evaluating what isn't working in your life – the relationships, activities, and situations that drain your energy – and reduce or eliminate them. Afterward, you have a clean slate from which to add experiences and relationships that appeal to you, trying them on for size and evaluating what makes you happy.

The key to making these improvements stick long-term is to evaluate the root of your dissatisfaction or joy in each. When you know why you like or dislike something, you can better understand the consequences of allowing similar changes in the future. Living your dream is a lifelong process, one that changes over time, and cultivating a habit of eliminating the negatives and adding in the positives will serve you well as you continue to refine your life.

In the next chapter you'll learn how to define the dream you have taking shape, visualize it so well you can put a price tag on it and begin the actions necessary to make it real.

Chapter 2: Make It Real

"Whatever you do, or dream you can, begin it.
Boldness has genius and power and magic in it."

— Johan Wolfgang von Goethe

It wasn't until 2007, when my 35-year-old brother had a heart attack, that we got our first inkling of our own mortality. Then in 2008 our good friend Maria had a brain aneurysm in her 30s, and we were completely thrown. We discovered in an instant how our plans could so easily be shattered by forces beyond our control. Life truly is short, and this wakeup call is what sped up our timeline for living our dream.

We had been spending all our time working and planning for a comfy retirement, and these two events showed us that so much was out of our control, most of all *time*. We did not have the guarantee of time to live out our dreams in retirement even if we worked and saved all our lives according to plan.

What's the solution? Well, you take advantage of the most precious resource first. That resource is time.

It took a pitcher of margaritas for us to make that discovery.

We were at El Camino, our favorite Mexican food restaurant in Seattle, with two good friends enjoying our second – or maybe fourth? – margarita on a long holiday weekend. We had been there for hours, talking about everything under the sun like good friends do when the weather is balmy and there is no work the next day.

Our mutual friend Maria was still in the hospital after suffering her brain aneurysm a month before and we didn't know what the future would hold for her. We couldn't help but think of my brother and his heart attack a year earlier and how much it had changed his life. Our friends had similar stories in their families of sudden illness and death.

We didn't know what the future held for any of us. As the night wore on and the margaritas flowed, we became a little more reflective and open about our fears. Could the same thing happen to any of us? Of course it could. We were then both 37, with good careers, nice financial prospects for the future, and a "plan," but the same could be said of my brother and Maria.

In fact, having a "plan" is what comforted us all along, let us know that we had things under control and were responsible adults. We had retirement savings. We even had a small savings account. After aggressively paying off our credit cards, we only had our mortgage as debt. We both had stable, well-paying careers and a home. Our plan was to retire early and travel extensively. But now we were faced with the previously unseen problem of not knowing how much time we actually had on this planet. Time is the wild card.

As it neared midnight, we asked the question that was on all of our minds:

"If you knew you wouldn't make it to your 40th birthday, what would you do differently now?"

As the question went around the table and we all laughed and groaned at each other's comments and predictions, we could feel an energy swelling around us. There was something to this question, and it was scratching an itch we didn't even know we had.

Warren and I looked across the table at each other and the electricity flowed. We had an entire conversation with our eyes in just a second, and we knew without a doubt that we were going to change our lives. I can't explain how it happened or why, but I will never forget the spark of that moment, the second our lives changed completely.

In that instant, we knew we wanted to travel the world together, and sooner rather than later.

The rest of the night was spent joking and laughing about what we'd do on this imaginary journey, but as we kept stealing glances at each other we knew it was the start of something big.

The next morning we asked each other, "Were you serious about last night?" The answer was an emphatic yes, and we started planning our trip around the world that very day (after the Alka-Seltzer, of course).

The longer you invest in your current reality – with your time, attention, money, and habits – the harder it will be to pull up stakes and make the changes necessary to live your dream. Don't kid yourself that you'll do it later. Langston Hughes said it best: *"A dream deferred is a dream denied."*

What is Your Dream?

Can you define it in such a way that someone else can visualize it, imagine you living a day in it, or snap a picture of it? Be very specific.

You can estimate cost and build a budget around specific dreams. A fuzzy dream will always have a fuzzy price tag and be out of reach.

"I want to be a successful author" becomes "I want to write full-time for X months to finish my masterpiece and get a book deal." We can't guarantee you'll be a successful author, but we do know you have to finish the book to even have a shot. Negotiating a sabbatical from work or amassing enough money to quit can allow you to pursue this dream.

"I want to travel the world" becomes "I want to take X time off to budget backpack around X countries" or "I'd like to take one really fantastic luxury vacation every single year and these are my top five destinations." You can work with this kind of specific information.

"I want to start a business" becomes "I want to start a part-time side business this year and grow it to full-time status within 2 years and quit my day job." You can work out a timeline of ramping up your business and decreasing the hours at your current job until you reach your goal.

Think about it so you can uncover any hidden costs or timeline restrictions before we start estimating your overall savings goal. If you need help getting started, the questions below will help you flesh out the dream you have in greater detail.

Define your dream

What is your dream? C'mon, give us some detail here! The more specific you can be, the easier it is to make your dream a reality. Use the following questions to brainstorm your dream into a reality you can almost touch.

- What does a day in your dream life look like?
    - Where do you live?

A new place every 12-24 mon or a destination job w/ vacation time

- What activities do you do? *Run a business. Run. Hike. scuba. Adventure*
- What kind of people do you know? *Fellow adventurers*
- What kind of work or creative pursuit do you do? *An Encouraging tourst areas.*
- Who is there with you? *My boyfriend at sea. Animals.*

• What is different about this picture from the life you're living today? *1. Quit my job. 2. Find a place 3. Convince the bf.*

  - List the things that need to change in your current life to make this happen.

When you have a specific dream in mind, it is time to start fleshing out the details.

If you have a partner or supportive friend, it's best to work together on this next section. (We'll cover aligning your dream with your partner in the next chapter.) Sometimes you need a different perspective to help you see available solutions. Be a little crazy with this. Remember that it's just an exercise to get your mind working on your dream, and saying that you'll do something extreme like quit your job and sell all of your possessions to travel the world with a backpack doesn't necessarily mean you have to do it. (Though we can recommend it!) Give yourself permission to think crazy thoughts, suggest outlandish scenarios, and let your stream of consciousness thinking lead the way. Your solution is buried somewhere within the answers to these questions, and it will only come to the surface if you work at it.

Digging a little deeper

• Do I keep my job? *NO,*
  - If so, does it change in any way?
  - Can I take a sabbatical?
  - Can I work part-time?
• If not, do I need another source of income?

- For how long? *New source of income.*
- Where will it come from? *A business I enjoy*
- Will I be returning to my career at some point? *Most likely no.*
  - o How do I plan for that?

- What will I do about my credit card debt and outstanding loans? *N/A*
  - Can I pay them off? If so, how?
  - Can I negotiate for better interest rates?
  - Can I get a deferment on paying back my student loans?
- What happens to my home and belongings? *sell my storage unit*
  - Will I still live there, or do I need to sell or lease?
  - Should I downsize? Upsize?
  - Should I store my belongings or sell some of them?
  - Do I need my car(s)? Or a better/different one?
- Will I need health insurance, life insurance, trip insurance, or any other type of coverage for my dream? *how to live abroad*
  - How will I finance it? *Top/out Savings account*
- What will happen to my pension or retirement accounts during my dream?
- What will my family or dependents be doing? *Family is young*
  - What do I need to do to prepare them? *No dependents*
- Do I need to improve my health and fitness before embarking on my dream? *No*
  - How will I do that?
  - How long will it take to be physically ready? *I'm mobile*

- Do I need to purchase special equipment or supplies?
    - How soon do I need them?
    - Can I space out the purchases over time?
    - Can I buy them secondhand or barter?
- Do I need/want the help of other people to make this happen?
    - Who specifically do I need?
    - What specifically do I need from these people?
    - How will I get their help?

How does your dream look now? Can you see it taking on a bit of reality?

Rewrite your dream again in more detail. This is the version you'll use to estimate costs and start your savings plan.

Work through the questions, give some real thought to your dream and how you want to make it happen, and we'll show you, step-by-step, how to amass the cash to do it.

Chapter Summary

When you take your dream from fuzzy to clear you can begin to imagine the components and actions necessary to make it real. This clarity can come from simply imagining a day in the life of your dream and breaking out the components. To make X happen, you need to do Y and Z, for example. This is a great exercise in determining the parts of your dream you really want and the ones that might not be so great on further examination.

Once you have your dream firmly in mind, clear as a picture, write it down in detail. This is the working goal of your Action Plan and will help you determine the cost and the actions necessary to make it come true.

It helps to have a supportive friend or mate work with you on the ideal vision because they can often point out opportunities and potential questions you don't see yet. There are also some problems in working with another person on this, especially a mate, and we'll cover those in the next chapter. If you're single, you can feel free to skip directly to Chapter 4.

Chapter 3: Align with Your Partner

"No two on earth in all things can agree. All have some daring singularity."

~ Winston Churchill

What happens next is usually one of two things if you're part of a couple: either "I can't wait to do this with you!" or "You want to do WHAT?"

If you are partnered or married, you are probably wondering right now how to align your dream with your mate. Not every couple is on the same page when it comes to their dreams. In fact, we were both married before so we know what it's like to be in sync as well as what it's like to be on Mars and Venus. What we didn't know way back then was how to travel through space to live a hot and happy life together on another planet.

If you and your partner have different dreams, or even the same dream but with different scenarios, then you have a bit of work to do before we move on. There is no answer to "how can I make my spouse share my dream?" because you're not in love with a robot. You can't make someone share your goals and dreams. Your partner is human, just like you, with his or her own wants, needs, fears and motivations.

There is hope, however. 'Principled negotiation' is the term coined by Roger Fisher and William Ury in the 1981 landmark book, *Getting to Yes*. There are 4 components:

- Separate the people from the problem
- Focus on interests, not positions
- Invent options for mutual gain
- Insist on objective criteria

World leaders, titans of industry, and even the police hostage negotiators use these methods in hammering out difficult situations, so it is certainly powerful enough for your relationship. Let's take a look to see how you can use principled negotiation to align with your partner.

Separate the People from the Problem

There is a reason we hire lawyers to fight things out: they aren't emotionally involved. They won't be tempted to dredge up events from the past, cry, throw things, or call names. They only see the problem in front of them and dispassionately work on a solution to the problem.

We certainly don't advocate getting an attorney involved in the negotiation of your dream with your partner, but it is helpful to realize why a dispassionate approach is so beneficial. You can't remove yourself entirely from the problem, but you can give yourself a lot of distance if you work at it. When you don't have a personal agenda, you are more likely to listen when your mate is speaking than just impatiently waiting for your turn. This listening is what helps you see things from his or her vantage point, which is key in coming up with a mutually beneficial solution.

When he wants to buy a big-screen television and you want to live in a TV-free house, there is some ground to cover. You can't think of him as a couch potato who is trying to ignore you and he can't think of you as a nag who's trying to take away his only relaxation. Why do you want time away from the television? Why does he feel the need to check out so completely? The answer to your problem lies with these 2 questions, not how you feel when you don't get your way.

Remember, this is a problem to be solved and not a personal attack. The only way to have a successful outcome is to create a solution that resolves the problem for both of you. Focus on the problem of being out of alignment in your dreams and how to fix it, not on the blame of how you got here.

Focus on Interests, Not Positions

When you come into a negotiation with an outcome in mind, it really isn't a negotiation. You have an agenda, and you're there to push it through. If your mate feels the same way, you're at a standstill before you even begin. People often take extreme positions without considering why and whether it will actually achieve their interests. Will a bigger house make you feel more secure? Maybe at first, but if you can't really afford it, your dream house can actually make you less secure as you struggle to keep up with the payments. If you instead focus on how to feel more secure, you and your partner can come up with a solution that won't break the bank or cause you greater anxiety in the future.

Focus on the feeling you want to have in your dream life instead of how you think it will look. Craving adventure, creativity, love, tranquility, security, vitality and confidence are all worthy interests with thousands of ways to make them come true. By focusing only on these interests, you can work with your partner to figure out the best way to get there.

Invent Options for Mutual Gain

If you're going to be living this dream together, make sure you both want it. If you've separated your personal issues from the problem and come into the negotiation with your interests instead of an outcome in mind, you are in a great place to invent options for mutual gain. It's not a win-lose situation (and if it is, then you both lose in the end).

If you've laid out your interests to the imaginary attorney from earlier in the chapter, what options would she bring to the table for you? Remember, she has no vested interest in your relationship, so she's going to bring offers you might not even consider on your own.

Let's say you want more adventure in your life but your partner is a diehard sports nut who is tied to the games on television every week. How would your imaginary attorney lay out the options for you? One idea is to merge what he likes to do with your goal of more adventure. If he loves baseball, you could create a shared dream of seeing a game in every professional baseball stadium in the world. Of course those trips will entail seeing the other local sights while you're there and enjoying new foods and activities, so you both get what you want as a team. The situation just went from 2 separate dreams to a mutual goal you can pursue together. Your imaginary lawyer is a genius.

There is a lot of value in imagining how a dispassionate observer or someone you admire would solve a problem. It takes you out of your own way and allows you to be creative in a way you sometimes can't by yourself.

If you are a single person, it helps to challenge yourself with a hypothetical question. One friend told us she imagines "What would Warren and Betsy do?" when an unusual opportunity arises. She admires our adventurous spirit, and it helps her to better gauge her own self-imposed limitations by putting the problem to our imaginary selves. We do the same thing using our imaginary mentors when we're facing a challenging decision. It is a great exercise in realizing your self-imposed psychological limitations and challenging yourself to overcome them.

Insist on Objective Criteria

You could call this the fairness factor. Is the solution you came up with fair and reasonable? We'll spend the next several chapters working out the feasibility of your idea from the financial, emotional, and social standpoints. But before you walk away from your dream negotiation you should intrinsically feel like you are in alignment with your partner and excited about the agreement on how you both envision your dream life.

If you aren't, it's time to go back to the drawing board, because what follows demands a strong team. If you aren't in alignment from the start, you'll never reach the finish line.

Creating a Family Goal

Let's learn how Matt took his solo dream and made it a family project. Matt told us he wanted to take his family to Indonesia for a one-year sabbatical. His wife is Indonesian, and he wanted his two sons to have more contact with their heritage. He also wanted a break from the frenetic pace of his job while his kids were still young. He knew the break would offer them some much-needed family time as well as the space to figure out another way of living to give them more time together.

Matt said, "We are all going to die. The older I get the more this thought haunts me. We get one shot at this life. Am I doing the things I dream about or is the fear of uncertainty pulling the strings?"

Matt set out to make this dream a reality by announcing the goal, starting up a website, and beginning sabbatical negotiations with his company. He was all set to make this a reality, charging full steam ahead to make it happen. He thought his wife would be overjoyed at the prospect of returning to Indonesia for an extended visit (which she was), but he did not anticipate the insecurity she felt over what would happen to their house, the kids' schooling, or their long-term financial security. She wanted to make him happy, but to say this was a shared dream would be an overstatement. The kids felt their parents' disconnect (don't they always?), and because they hadn't bought into the dream they only worried about leaving their friends behind.

As time went by, Matt found it more difficult to save money and make the changes necessary for the sabbatical. Unexpected expenses kept coming in because they didn't plan for them as a family. He was frustrated, and the dream quickly dissolved into nothing. He says, "We failed miserably. I felt like I had not only let myself down but everyone who supported our dream. I hated myself and my life. I stopped blogging, sank into depression, argued and fought with my family and mentally surrendered to the thought that this was how my life was supposed to be. I felt trapped, unable to escape a situation that didn't appeal to me. I had no clear picture of what it was I really wanted."

Matt's a smart guy, so he didn't stay down for long. He bought a copy of this book and realized the error in trying to make his dream happen for everyone. He and his wife sat down for a heart-to-heart talk. They went about recalibrating their goals into something they could achieve as a family. The new sabbatical timeline was shorter, a better option was found at work, and the family gave themselves more time to come up with the cash. Everyone bought into it, even their sons, and it made saving and making lifestyle changes much easier. Matt no longer felt like the boss pushing his family into doing this, and the family felt like they were on a reasonable path to achieve a dream together. They made practical decisions about their belongings and renting out their home. They even started a couple of side businesses to bring in extra cash (more on this in Chapter 13).

Matt contacted us by email at this point, and it was a real treat to stay in touch with him over the next year as his family moved further along the path toward their dream. By addressing everyone's wants and concerns as a family, they were able to achieve their dream as a family. Matt and his family did make it to Indonesia, and with it came new opportunities they never imagined. We'll revisit Matt's story later in the book.

How to Start a Conversation about Dreams

The key to lining up your dreams starts with talking. But first you have to take out the judgment, the manipulation, the guilt, the fear, and the anger so you can have a logical discussion to learn what will eventually bring you together on an idea.

- **State** your specific dreams out loud to each other or write them down and read them to each other if you're nervous. This is not the time for mind reading. Be very explicit in what you want in your dream life. A great idea is to share your "ideal day" scenarios with each other.

- **Confirm** what your partner is saying she/he wants overall: less work, more time with you, more time to explore an interest, more excitement in life, less stress, etc. This is no time for guessing games, and you should each ask as many clarifying questions as you need. "What do you mean when you say ____?" "What would that look like?" "Can you give me an example?" "I took that to mean____." State back to each other what you understand the other one wants until you get it. (This process helps your partner solidify their wants as much as it clarifies them for you.)

- **List** all of the overall similarities in your dreams, ignoring the specifics on how to get there (you both want more free time or a change in location or opportunities to learn). You should start feeling a little sizzle right now as the possibilities start lining up, maybe even options you never considered before.

- **Identify** the gap between your interests. How can you bridge it? Maybe one of you wants to take a year off to travel the world via backpack while the other wants an extended luxury vacation every year. Those goals are not as far apart as they seem, and a little honest conversation – it is the same overall goal of exploration and enjoyment, isn't it? – will bring you to a solution that gives you both what you want.

This is a very exciting time for most people because it is a new way of negotiating in a relationship. On top of that, you are negotiating on dreams and fulfillment, not the usual 'discussions' around paying bills or whose family to visit at the holidays. It's a great strategy to learn because you can use it over and over again in your relationship, bypassing most of the guilt and blame in your arguments and getting right down to the problem resolution. This is probably not a conversation that will bring alignment in 10 minutes, but it is one that will open up the lines of communication to find that perfect solution for you if you keep at it.

Be open-minded

We talked before about your dream morphing over time. Life is ripe with change as we grow, and this open communication you now have with your partner will insure you can manage the changes and opportunities you discover along the way. Even though Warren and I are on the same page when it comes to traveling around the world, we are not always on the same page about how to do it. In fact, our dream lifestyle has undergone some change even as we've lived it, and yours probably will, too.

We initially agreed to backpack around the world on a moderate budget, but neither one of us wanted to 'rough it' on a regular basis. We wanted private rooms and bathrooms. We enjoyed good food and conversation. And in our 40s, we wanted a comfy bed to sleep in every night. So our version of budget travel is probably different than a 20-something student on a gap year trip, but we had to flesh out what a day in our dream life looked like so we could decide if it was right for us.

As we've traveled, we've learned that speed is the enemy to our enjoyment of the trip and the spark to a short fuse with each other. We've slowed our pace even more than we initially imagined, and for the most part we are living as temporary ex-pats in countries around the world more than travelers. Our life is different than what we initially imagined, but because we've kept our communication clear we've been able to consistently negotiate all the way through. You'll need this skill, too, because the dream you come up with in the following chapters is going to change over time. This is one thing we can guarantee, so before we go a step further we just want to emphasize the importance of forming a collaborative team with your mate and keeping the lines of communication open.

You love your partner. Your partner loves you. You want to be together and make each other happy. There is harmony somewhere in all of that. The outcomes you achieve through communication, sharing and open-mindedness will lead you towards a dream life with your partner, which is the sweetest reward of all. (We'll talk more about alignment as we create the budget Roadmap.)

Chapter Summary

If you are in a relationship or a family, your dream impacts those around you. In rare instances you'll be in total alignment, but for the vast majority of people there is some negotiation to be done.

Instead of bemoaning why your mate doesn't want you to be happy (which isn't true), instead learn the art of principled negotiation, where the outcome of shared interests is more important than your position going in. By focusing on the dreams you both share – a feeling or state of being currently being expressed in different ways – you can find alignment to create a mutual goal.

If it is too hard for you to see your options together, imagine what a disinterested third party leading your negotiation would suggest. Sometimes you have to take yourself out of the situation to see it clearly. Once you open the lines of communication with your mate, keep them open. One thing you can count on in this life is it will change, and the key to managing it is being honest and open with your mate.

In the next chapter we'll take your dream and create some motivation around it, even giving it the grand name it deserves. Whether you are working alone or with a partner, this next step is going to be insanely fun.

Chapter 4: Create Your Dream Porn

"You must have long term goals to keep you from being frustrated by short term failures."

~Charles C. Noble

Do you remember the giant roll-down maps from grade school? They worked just like window shades, except on much heavier paper and longer rods. My sixth-grade teacher Mrs. Stewart would use a hook on a stick to reach up to the top of the chalkboard to pull down maps of the US and the world, depending on the subject we were studying at the time. As kids we liked to imagine students just like us studying geography in places like China or South America. I still associate maps and travel with the smell of chalk.

When it came to motivating us about our dream we instantly wanted one of those giant schoolroom maps for our house. We began scouting our area for one and found it in a local map shop. We raced home to pin it to our wall and then stepped back to take it all in. We had the *whole world* right in front of us.

Over the next 2 years we spent hours in front of it, tracing out imaginary journeys, boning up on our rusty geographic knowledge, and dreaming of how much of the world we'd be able to see. We learned about latitude and longitude and topography and discovered the real Tropic of Cancer, which was far less scandalous than Henry Miller's book of the same name. We learned that Timbuktu is in Western Africa and Inner Mongolia is really part of China. This map allowed us to rediscover the world and imagine ourselves traveling in it.

We hung this map in the front room of our home. It reminded us every time we entered and left our home why we were working so hard to make our dream come true. It was a talking point with visitors to our home, and we even filmed a few videos in front of it for our website. In fact, we began calling it our Dream Porn because it really did stimulate us to action!

> *Dream Porn is your big motivator, the reminder you place in a prominent space to keep your goal front and center. You will need this reminder on the days when you're weak, tired, or feeling a lot of peer pressure to spend.*

One of our smartest strategies was setting up our Craigslist 'staging area' for selling all our possessions in the same room as our Dream Porn. When people came to buy things from us it sparked a conversation about why we were selling, and many people felt compelled to help us on our quest by buying more things! (Don't worry; you don't have to sell all your belongings to make your dream come true. This was simply part of our dream of being unencumbered as we traveled. But if you want help decluttering your life and making some extra cash, check out our book, *Getting Rid of It: Eliminate the Clutter from Your Life*.)

The map story shows why reminders are important. It is why we leave ourselves Post-it notes, set the things we don't want to forget to take with us by the door the night before, and even put our exercise clothes at the foot of the bed to encourage us to work out when we first get up. (Well, I'm sure at least a few people do that last one.)

This huge reminder of your dream, what you're going to spend the near future working toward every single day, is a big motivator to stick to your savings plan. You don't necessarily have to be cheeky and call it Dream Porn like we do, but you do need to indulge in this bit of mental self-pleasure on a regular basis to keep yourself focused on your main desires while all those nagging little wants – which are easier to get – are begging for your attention.

Our Dream Porn sent a message to us as well as every person who came to our house, whether to socialize or to pick up an item they bought online, that we had a big goal. It was a regular, everyday reminder of why we were doing this thing, what we could look forward to in a relatively short period of time, and a deterrent for continuing habits that would keep us mired in our current situation. It was hard to come into our house with bags from shopping and not immediately regret purchases outside our budget when we saw the map.

Not every bit of motivation is visual, of course. The map was our primary source of motivation, but we also learned to cook exotic foods through recipes we found online, watched foreign films with subtitles, listened to world music on our iPods, and practiced our Spanish with the free Coffee Break Spanish podcast from the Radio Lingua Network (we planned to go to South America first). Every day had a little bit of our dream in it, so it was more difficult to fall off the wagon when it came to our savings plan. It was no longer this far-off dream; we were thinking about it, seeing it, smelling it, hearing it and eating it every single day.

Making your dream part of your everyday life is key to maintaining your motivation for change. If you're thinking about your dream every single day, it will become easier to save money, create new habits, and see opportunities.

Creating Your Dream Porn

Beth Hayden used Dream Porn as part of her plan to stop living a double life. In the daytime, she was a mild-mannered administrative assistant at a tech company. She booked travel, compiled expense reports, and took minutes. She even made the coffee. But on her lunch breaks and after hours, she was a hustling entrepreneur, building websites for small businesses and showing them how to use social media. She longed to ditch her day job and become her own boss, but as a single mother she needed a steady income. She didn't know how find the time to build her 4-year-old business without quitting her job, and she couldn't quit her job without more money from her business. She was in a tough spot.

We caught up with Beth via Skype while we were in China and she was promoting her first book. It was a long way for all of us from our first email exchange just a year before. You see, Beth was the very first buyer of our book, and the thank you email I sent her sparked an online friendship. We were privy to her entire experience working through *Dream Save Do*, and we really enjoyed watching her dream unfold. We think you will, too.

Beth told us she bought *Dream Save Do* and "tore through [it] like a starving woman, knowing deep down that I was looking for a way to save my own life — a way to stop feeling dead inside every day when I trudged into the office and sat through endless meetings discussing things I didn't care about."

Beth's first step was to create her Dream Porn, a board of images designed to inspire and motivate her toward her dream life. She cut out images and phrases from magazines to represent the kind of life she wanted to live, a life with adventure, fulfilling work, love, fun and travel with her son. She put them together as a collage on a giant poster board and then hung it on the wall in her home. She saw this poster every single day, and it motivated her to make the changes necessary to make her dream happen. We'll revisit Beth's story later in the book.

What kind of dream porn do you like? The choices are endless, depending on your goal and your sensory desires:

- **Smell** A friend loves Maui and wants to live there eventually. When I think of Maui, I think of the specific scent of gardenias. It was the defining scent of Hawaii during our travels there, including the soap in the bathroom at our guesthouse. We can never smell gardenias without thinking of Maui. Get yourself a "scent-sual" reminder of your dream in the form of soaps, candles, teas or spices.

- **Hear** Music, anyone? After traveling in South America, we can be instantly transported back to the Andes Mountains with the sound of a pan flute or the radio-friendly love songs of Colombian superstar Juanes. You may feel the same way about the music of a specific place, the songs of a happier time in your life when you were actively following your dreams, or the type of music that helps you create more of what you hope to do when you reach your dream. Consider a Dream Porn Soundtrack (the boom chicka wow-wow of your dreams!) to keep you motivated every day. You can create and old-school mix tape, a playlist in iTunes for your iPod, or check the thousands of streaming radio stations online for the type of music you want.

- **See** Create a vision board for your dream like Beth did or drive by and take a picture of the exact location you want to live in or the place you want to start your new business. Put it on your wall, your refrigerator, your desk at work, and your bathroom mirror. You can even make a Pinterest2 board if you want to share it with others. The critical point is to make sure you can see it every day.

- **Taste** Food can transport you to another world – perhaps even your dream world. If you want to live in another place, regularly cook those foods and use those spices. If you want to open a restaurant, prepare the kind of meals you want to serve in the way you want to serve them. You get bonus points here because you can smell it while it's cooking and then eat your inspiration.

- **Touch** Sometimes you need to hold it in your hand. When I was writing my first novel, I created a mock cover for it with a blurb on the outside that said "New York Times Bestseller!" and a back cover with my photo and bio. I wrapped it around a "real" book and kept it propped up on my desk to see as I wrote. It helped me finish the book and – more importantly – start thinking of myself as a writer. This could also work for your invention, product, or idea. A friend who wants to move to Vienna uses a planner with a Viennese theme so she can see it every day. Seeing it in real life – even as a mock-up – can be a huge motivator.

Dream Porn creates a bit of realism to anchor your dream-ism. It will be a subtle reminder every single day of why you're working so hard to save and denying yourself those little pleasures that do nothing to bring you closer to your dream.

What will you use for motivation every day?

Don't discount the power of Dream Porn. And for goodness' sake don't hide it under your bed!

Name Your Dream

Now that you have one or more pieces of motivation, it's time to make this dream official. The way we do that is to give it a name.

When you name something, it bestows power, substance and identity.

In ancient times, knowing an enemy's name gave you power over him. In one famous tale, a foolish miller brags to a king that his daughter can spin straw into gold. In a not-so-surprising move, the king asks her to demonstrate her skill. She's locked in a room with hay and instructed to fill it to the ceiling with gold by morning, which terrifies her since she doesn't know how to spin at all. An imp comes to her rescue by telling her he will do it in exchange for her necklace. She gladly gives it to him, and he spins the straw into gold. The king is delighted and moves her to an even bigger room filled with hay, asking it to be filled with gold by the next morning. Again she is saved by the imp, who spins the gold in exchange for her ring. Finally the girl is taken to an enormous room, and the king promises to marry her if she can fill it with gold but will kill her if she cannot. The imp returns, but she has nothing left to offer in exchange for his help. He makes a deal with her to take her first-born child, an offer she foolishly accepts.

Once the girl became queen, she quickly became pregnant and had a baby. The imp returned to collect his due, and she begged him to take anything else but her firstborn child. She offered him all the riches in the kingdom, but he declined. He did make a bargain with her, though. He said if she could guess his real name when he returned 3 days hence he would let her keep her baby. The queen had the imp followed, and as he danced a jig in the forest that night he sang out his name: Rumpelstiltskin. The messenger hurried back to the queen, who played dumb when the imp returned 3 days later but finally spat out his name, sending him into a fit of fury. He had no choice but to leave empty-handed. By knowing his name, she gained control over him.

In modern times names are used as shorthand to communicate. (I call myself Betsy instead of The Eldest Freckled Daughter of House Gray, though reading *Game of Thrones* is making me rethink this decision.) We also assign names (and nicknames) to show affection. People name everything from their pets to their cars to their computers. Bestowing names is an indication of love, ownership, and a way to share them with others. Since you will love, own, and share your dream with others, it also needs a name.

When you give your dream a name, you make it easier to manage yourself as well as for others to step in and help, offer guidance, and make it better or easier than you could on your own. In Beth's case, she boldly named her dream The Free Bethy Project. Her day job felt like a prison to her, and the emotion she wanted to feel upon achieving her dream was freedom. She was smart to focus on the end result and not on the work needed to get there (*Bethy's 80-Hour Work Week* would not have been nearly as motivational.)

She announced the name on her business website and was floored to discover most of her clients and peers didn't even know she had a day job! They heaped encouragement on her in the form of comments, emails and phone calls, and it set the mood for the burst of activity she used to grow her business. This was a bold move for publicizing her dream and passively enlisting help from others (more on that in Chapter 15), and it gave her an incredible amount of motivation right at the starting gate.

You don't need a blog¹ to announce your dream's name, but you will be telling people about it and a great name will convey your enthusiasm and seriousness about your goal. Claiming ownership and naming rights also give you power over your dream, just like the queen had with Rumpelstiltskin.

How to Name Your Dream

This isn't the time to go small. It's your dream, after all, and probably a big departure from your existing way of living. So give it a grand name worthy of the effort:

- *The Massive Brain Investment 2014* for your savings plan to return to college
- *The Healthy Happy Heart Hour* for your new daily exercise commitment
- *The Midlife Get a Life Plan of 2013* for your goal of trying a new hobby or activity every month of the year
- *The Smith Castle of 2015* for your goal of buying a home
- *Sexy Summer Streamlining Strategy* for your goal of cleaning out the clutter in your life this summer

- *The Free Me by 2015 Project* for your goal of becoming self-employed by a certain date

Notice the similarities in these examples. They all contain a descriptor and a unit of time. This is important, because dreams without deadlines rarely become reality. We'll be talking more about setting dates and timelines in chapter 6, so if you want to hold off on the date until then that's okay. Just remember you'll need one.

The other consideration is to make your dream's name something you can share with other people. This will make it more fun to share with your friends, who will want to help and can ask about your progress using dream's your name.

To create your dream's name:

- Think in terms of the result or feeling you want, not the work it takes to get there. You'll be far more motivated by envisioning your happy ending than you will by reminding yourself of the work remaining. Make it easy to feel good when you say your dream's name.
- Put a date or timeframe around it. When you add a date to your name you give it a sense of urgency. It's not some far-off dream; it's just around corner and you'd better get to it if you want it to happen on time.
- Be grand and use adjectives. Hey, this is your dream we're talking about. Why wouldn't you name it with the same kind of love and creativity you used to name your pets or your children? Make your dream's name fun or fantastic to say. You should enjoy saying it out loud and sharing it with other people.

Remember, once you name a dream, you bring it to life and claim ownership. It's now up to you to feed it and care for it until it is grown.

A Final Word on Motivation

When people think of changing their lives, they often daydream about the big moment, the point where they cease living the everyday and begin living their version of the good life. It is a lottery-winner mindset, one that says, *"until X happens, I won't be living my dream."*

If you think of your own dreams this way, waiting for something to happen to show you that your dream is finally real, I'd like to challenge you to try something new – something revolutionary, in fact.

Stop imagining your dream as a full-grown adult and see it as an infant, waiting to be nurtured by you every hour of every day until it is ready to stand on it's own.

A funny thing happens when you envision your dream as a baby instead of an adult. You stop expecting the dream to work for you and begin doing the necessary work for the dream. The mind shift is subtle but profound, and by realistically seeing the status of your dreams – and the work needed to make them reality – you'll see far more of them reach productive adulthood.

Chapter Summary

Any dream worth having takes some time to create, and it is only natural that your motivation will lag at some point. To keep yourself on track toward your dream, it is important to create some sort of Dream Porn to remind you of your goal. You can do this visually with dream boards or maps, or you can focus on any or all of the senses to keep your dream a daily part of your life. It is much easier to stay on track with your dream if it is a big part of your current life.

Another powerful motivator is to name your dream. When you give it a name, you give it life and claim ownership. This is a potent step and one that will make sharing your dream with others easier and more fun than explaining it to them step by step. It also gives you a piece of shorthand to use when talking about your dream with others.

Finally, learn to see your dream as the infant it is. In order to make it into the full-grown life of your dreams, it will take daily nourishment and action. By giving yourself the motivation to work for it every single day, you'll become the best parent you can be to your fledgling little dream.

In the next chapter we'll start pricing this baby out, figuring out the actual amount needed to make it happen. We'll also start talking about the daily habits you'll need to create to be ready for your dream when your financial goal is met.

Chapter 5: Put a Number on It

"By recording your dreams and goals on paper, you set in motion the process of becoming the person you most want to be."

~Mark Victor Hansen

Congratulations, you have defined your dream, aligned with your mate, and packaged it up nicely with a pithy name and a tasteful display of Dream Porn. That and $4 will buy you a grande latte at Starbucks.

We're not being flip; we're being real. Your dream won't go far – in fact, won't go anywhere – without some action on your part. This is where we separate the wannabes from the doers, from those who talk about their dreams to those who live them. This is where things get real.

After the high of making our decision and buying our map leveled off, we were faced with figuring out how much it would take to make the dream happen. It quickly brought us back to reality and our mothers' admonitions from childhood that "money doesn't grow on trees." Not only did we wonder where we were going to get the money to travel, we didn't even know how much to get!

Our dream at the time was to travel the world for one year. Besides figuring out how to save this unknown amount of money, we had to determine where to go, in what style of travel, and what to do with our home, possessions, and careers in the meantime. There were a lot of moving parts to this dream.

Just like our dream, you won't find yours sitting on a shelf at a store with a price tag on it. (And if you think you will, we need to have another conversation.) Much like you have to create it yourself, you also have to price it yourself. Time to roll up your sleeves and get down to business. (You're starting to get the idea that "action" is a key part of this book, right?)

Let's start with the dream you stated before. Maybe you want to become a painter, start a business, or buy a home. Maybe you even want to start a family or go back to school. Whatever the dream, you know it will cost you some money, either in the cost of doing it or purchasing it or by paying for your living expenses while you pursue it. You also know it will take some changes in your personal life to make it happen. You'll have to make decisions. You'll have to develop new habits and skills and let go of some that are standing in your way. It's all about choice, and when you choose to make a change to your life you're choosing not to continue things as they are.

It may sound obvious, but to a lot of people it isn't. To change your life, you have to actually *change* your life. That means a new way of looking at how you live, earn your money, save your money, interact in your relationships, and spend your free time. You don't get something for nothing.

We can't tell you how many times people have told us they want to change their lives in some significant way – but only if they don't have to change anything else. It doesn't work that way. When you decide to do something different with your life, you have to actually do something different with your life. There is no way around it. So now that we have that straight, let's start on your Action Plan. How are you going to get from where you are now to where you want to be?

Determine the Cost

The first step is to determine what it will cost. This number is often what drives the timeline for the other activities in support of your dream. It is also what keeps so many people from starting their dreams.

The morning after we decided to take this one-year trip around the world we had no idea how much it would cost. In fact, the first guess in my head was $1 million – a sum I didn't think we could ever reach. We didn't know anyone who had done something similar, so we had no benchmark to help us create our own budget. We went back and forth for a while wondering about the cost, pulling numbers out of the air like they meant something. If we hadn't gone the extra step of actually putting a price tag on our dream we would likely still be sitting at our kitchen table mulling over the idea of travel...some day.

Price it like a pro

Even if you don't know anyone personally who has done what you want to do, there is someone out there who has. Google is your friend, and you can use it to find examples of people who have already done this thing you so want to do. We were astounded to find dozens of people documenting their world travels online, and even a few of them including costs. We found people traveling in luxury style, others sleeping on hammocks in beaches, and still others mapping out a version somewhere in the middle. I think most of all we were just shocked to find this subculture of people already doing what we thought was so shocking and new. You might find the same with your dream.

These examples encouraged us to ask the right questions to find our own price tag:

- At what luxury level do we want to travel?
- How fast do we want to travel?
- Where do we want to travel?

By answering these 3 questions (moderate budget, slowly, in South America to start), we were able to calculate a realistic price tag for our dream. It helped us find estimates for lodging, transportation, and food as well as entertainment. Our original budget from September 2008 estimated we'd spend $100/day to travel the world.

It is always better to average up on your savings goals rather than down. Don't assume you'll be able to work out better deals or count on a financial windfall. Bet on the sure money and make your estimates from there. Any additional funds or cost savings are just icing on the cake to speed up your timeline.

How to price your dream

Do you know how much this dream will cost? If it's buying a car or home, you can pretty easily figure out what you need in terms of purchase price, maintenance, insurance, and fuel or utilities. Sales prices are available online, and you can easily estimate the other expenses with online calculators.

School, traveling, or writing a book might be a little trickier because you'll need to figure out your living expenses along the way. Starting a business will require a bit of research to come up with a number. This is where you can start spiraling out of control and getting lost in the process. If you think your dream is super special or has all kinds of details to figure out first, you're shooting yourself in the foot before the race. It is very important you don't get hung up on the planning or you will never get started on the action, and that's what's going to make your dream come true.

Figuring out the cost of your dream is the first potential sinkhole in your path to saving. We already know what you're going to tell us. Your dream is really complicated and you need time to figure it all out. Or you're different from everyone else because you have X, Y, and Z to consider. Or you don't have any spare money at the moment so it doesn't make any sense to figure this out until you do.

Bullshit.

That was us calling you on it before you even have time to get the excuse out of your mouth. We do this out of love, of course, and because we know human nature. We did the same things, and because we've already been down this path we're pointing out the potholes to you. (*You're welcome.*)

Your dream has a price tag, one you can pretty accurately estimate in less than a day. In fact, we're going to challenge you to estimate it in less than an hour by focusing your energies.

Let us introduce you to Samantha. She dreamed of opening her own specialty cake business from the moment she baked her first fancy cake. The response was enthusiastic, and she knew she had a talent. Moms from all over the neighborhood called weeks in advance to get her birthday and special-occasion cakes. It became so expensive for her to bake these cakes she finally had to start saying no, despite her love of it.

What kept her from starting her own business and setting the date was her own assumption about starting a business. As the wife of a police officer in rural Australia, she and her husband were living in government-sponsored housing. She didn't think the rules would allow her to run a commercial kitchen out of her house, so she simply put her dream on the back burner until the day they would finally move.

Sam shared her story with us over Skype from Australia. She said the confidence boost she gained from reading our website pushed her to stop talking about it and finally put this dream to rest. She'd either find out for sure she couldn't start a food business in her house or she'd learn what it took to make it happen. She made a few calls and was stunned to find out it was not only permissible, but an inspection and a short certification course was all she needed to be up and running. She began estimating the costs and the few pieces of equipment she would need to buy, and she was off and running to make her dream a reality.

Quick estimates

In order to avoid the first sinkhole, we're going to set a timer: 15 minutes. Yes, 15 minutes. You quickly map out the estimated expenses for the dream you defined and come up with a nice round number at the end. Don't worry if you're not right; you won't be. But you also won't be right if you spend weeks working out every single line item. If you've ever taken a vacation or done a home remodeling project, you know what we mean.

The important thing right here is to get a good starting number as well as documenting the variables to your dream, the things you can modify on the path to making it come true. Once you have that down, you can go back and revise the numbers to your heart's content – but not before. Trust us on this.

Remember, any activity that keeps you from taking action on your dream is the enemy.

Let us repeat: Any activity that keeps you from taking action on your dream is the enemy. Action is key.

So, what kind of research are we talking about?

Do you need to save 10% of the purchase price of a home for a down payment?

Do a quick scan of the real estate ads to find a home in your desired area and in your price range. It doesn't have to be the perfect home with the right light fixtures, just an average home in your desired budget and location. Calculate from there to get your 10%. Done.

Are you planning to go back to college?

Plan for what you need based on the stated rates, not what you think you might get in scholarships or government funding. That's an adjustment you'll be happy to make later. University websites and catalogs make this pretty easy to calculate. Done.

Would you like to travel long-term?

Defining the area of travel makes it pretty easy to calculate a cost. You know that South America will be cheaper than Europe and peak season means higher rates everywhere. You can even cheat a little on this one since we publish a monthly expense report of our travels. Come up with your ballpark number and refine it later.

You can continue doing this for your new business, an invention, setting aside time to write your novel or start painting/photography as a full-time pursuit. You can even map out your savings goal for starting a family.

(Funny side note: we have a few friends who have either adopted or had in-vitro fertilization to start their families.

We've heard them each joke that their children are not priceless; they know exactly how much it cost to get them!)

You can also use the estimating tools at Smarty Pig or Mint or MoneyDashboard to help you come up with your figures. All three services are free to join and take just minutes to organize your financial details and budget projections. We love using tools like this to plan because they are quick and allow users to test out various scenarios easily and get to the action phase much faster.

We'll be talking a lot about these 3 free services throughout the book:

- **SmartyPig** is a free online piggy bank for people in the US and Australia saving for specific financial goals.
- **Mint** brings all your financial accounts together online or on your mobile device, automatically categorizes your transactions, lets you set budgets, and helps you achieve your savings goals. Mint is available in the US and Canada.
- **MoneyDashboard** is a free online dashboard for UK users to access all your accounts in one place and manage your money.

How did we do our research? Well, it didn't take 15 minutes initially, and we quickly got bogged down and almost lost our momentum altogether. That's why we won't let it happen to you.

The morning after we made our decision to travel, we brewed a big pot of coffee and sat down at the kitchen table to start our research. We had no idea what it would cost, how much we could get for renting our house, or the expense of storing all our things. Like you, we had a million questions and very few answers.

As we read more travel blogs and looked up flights and hotels online, we became more worried and confused.

One person could travel in Asia on $5US per day and another in Europe on $250US per day, and both considered themselves budget travelers. Were they really traveling in the same style and the difference in price was solely due to location? Were we more like $5 guy or $250 guy?

Another couple spent $70,000US for 10 months of travel, but their blog showed pictures of them at swank resorts and they made a couple of trips back home to the US during their travels. We weren't going to do that, so how would that number change for us?

- How much would we rent our house for?
- Would we have enough left over to help fund our travel, or would we be paying the difference?
- How much would it cost to store all of our stuff?
- Man, is it better just to sell the whole lot of it?

We spent a couple of days knee deep in research, and finally we had enough.

There is no magic formula out there to tell you exactly how much your dream will cost just like there is no magic formula for living happily ever after.

There is only a suggested guideline based on other people's experience and then refining it for your personal tastes. Get comfortable with estimating it, because you're in uncharted territory, mapping out the path to your own brand of happiness.

We did just that by calculating the costs of the cheapest place we were likely to stay and the most expensive place we were likely to stay and a reasonable amount of transportation thrown in. When we completed all the calculations the estimate came in at $36,500 per year of travel, or $100/day, well below the *"don't we have to be millionaires to do that?"* number we had in mind at the beginning.

It is pretty scary how 'on' we were with that quick calculation. Even now, well after our first planning session and years into our trip around the world, we are still working off that same "daily average" number of $100/day we came up with at our final 15-minute planning session. You can see exactly how close we live to this number now with our monthly expense reports at www.RTWExpenses.com.

People instinctively know when they're getting the right info about their dream, and they only continue researching to either confirm it enough so there's no risk left (which will never happen) or because they cannot believe it is within reach.

It is.

I remember when we came up with the original estimate for our trip. It was a little disorienting at first. I mean, $36,500 was no small chunk of change, but it was an amount within reach, and by knowing that, we knew our goal was within our grasp.

Resources for your 15-minute research session

Google your dream

- Someone out there has done something similar to what you want, and you can learn from him or her.
- Note what is similar and dissimilar in your dreams.

- Scan for information instead of reading every word. You just want the costs, not the details, on living the dream. Bookmark all the relevant websites to review in detail later.

Tally the numbers

- Always round up. Not everyone keeps a close tally on spending, so the figures you research are probably low.
- Do you have additional costs based on your personal situation? Throw those in, too.
- Do you have any savings or extra income that can be applied to your dream? Great. Figure those in, too.

Refer to your "Day in the Life" exercise from Chapter 1

- Have you included the costs you need to live that day in the life?
- How have you resolved your current spending requirements?
- Home
- Car(s)
- Outstanding debts
- Ongoing responsibilities
- Can you free up any cash in the near future by eliminating some of your current spending requirements?

Don't get caught up in the research. Your number will continue to be refined over time, and once you analyze your expenses and start making deposits into The Vault you can spend as much time as you like playing with the numbers.

We're ball-parking it here, first to get a jump-start on the plan, and second to show you that action is a more powerful path to success than research. You can revise this number to your heart's content *after* you start saving.

We're winding up the timer now. Go!

Chapter Summary

Determining the components of your dream will guide you to a starting estimate. You can easily get bogged down in this process since there are as many variables to your dream as you can imagine, so the important thing is to work from basic details to get your starting number. Once you have it and start taking action toward saving money, you can go back and refine the number to your heart's content. Until you get that number in place, though, you won't have a compelling reason to put money in the bank.

Remember that someone out there has done exactly what you want to do or a fairly close version of it, and if it can be documented online is probably is. Use the Internet to search for other people living your dream so you can determine the components needed to make it come true. Then take those components and price them out.

Keep in mind there is no magic formula, and whatever number you choose will be wrong. Even if you spend 6 months figuring out the number, you'll still be wrong. So it is better to be almost right and take immediate action than to be slightly-more-almost-right and lose 6 months of work toward your dream.

In the next chapter we're going to use this estimate to help set the date for your dream. Deadlines are what compel action, and this is where the clock to reaching your dream starts.

Chapter 6: Set the Date

"An average person with average talent, ambition and education can outstrip the most brilliant genius in our society if that person has clear, focused goals."

~Brian Tracy

Now you have a number – and a number you can wrap your head around, at that. When you *know* what something costs, you know if you can afford it in the not-too-distant future, which means you can seriously contemplate having it. It's no longer something you dream about or wish for; it's a real possibility. And we've gotta be honest here: it can scare the crap out of you.

Marianne Williamson famously said, "Our deepest fear is not that we are inadequate. Our deepest fear is that we are powerful beyond measure." Truer words were never spoken.

Once you know how much it will take to reach your goal – and that it's within reasonable reach – you may find yourself quaking in your boots a little bit. Dreaming without action is safe, pleasant, and never requires you to actually do anything. Active pursuit of your dream is a little bit intoxicating, and you have to be prepared for the disorientation that sometimes comes along with it.

We were a little giddy at first, looking at our number and smiling. And you know what? We had already mentally psyched ourselves into a higher number before the research, so we made our first bold move.

We asked ourselves if we could stretch it a bit and save a budget for 2 years of travel. (Yes, you can do that!) As my wise brother Bo says, "If you're gonna be a bear, be a grizzly."

So we set our goal for 2 years of travel with the nice round number of $75,000 needed to achieve our dream. Before we got too cozy with that, though, we had to figure out a deadline. How long would it take for us to find, save and earn that kind of money?

A Dream Without a Deadline is Dead

You know what happens to a plan without a deadline, don't you? Of course you do; it never gets finished. We imagine there is a little purgatory of dreams where bold starts, good intentions, and best-laid plans go to fade away. It is probably filled with home exercise equipment and New Year's resolutions.

A deadline gives you the push you need to take action, move forward, and work toward a destination. Without it, your only incentive to get it done is your initial enthusiasm, and that will fade over time no matter how sexy your Dream Porn. Let us state this clearly: Without a deadline you will never reach your goal. You need a finish line, an end point, a light at the end of the tunnel – whatever symbol you choose – to motivate you to complete the tasks needed to get there.

You remember Beth. She set a deadline of 6 months to quit her job and work her side business full time, mainly because she was desperate to change her life and needed the push to make it happen. Often we create roadblocks where there aren't any, and recognizing you need to give yourself a little kick in the pants can set the pace to achieve your dream in record time.

Beth set an ambitious calendar of activities to grow her business and got to work right away. She was determined to meet her goal, and she researched all the ways she could drive more small business customers to her site for social media training and website design. One tactic was to pitch heavily researched articles on marketing and social media to influential websites. When the popular website Copyblogger accepted her article on how to use Pinterest for business, she saw her client list boom. The article went viral, and it soon caught the attention of an editor at Wiley & Sons. When Beth received the email from an editor asking if she wanted to write a book on Pinterest, she almost fell out of her chair. The request came just days shy of her 6-month deadline, and the advance she received from the publisher was an additional bonus to help smooth the transition to full-time entrepreneurship. She quit her job a day ahead of schedule and hasn't looked back.

This is the other thing you can count on with setting a date: it will push you to do the things you've been putting off, actions that open doors and reveal opportunities to making your dream happen bigger, better and faster than you imagined. But first you have to set the date.

Outside factors in calculating your date

When do you want to start living your dream? You want to start school at the beginning of a semester, travel in good weather, and make sure you stay at your job long enough to get your annual bonus or finish your big project. Adding these factors into your saving time will give you a deadline. It will also help you plan those other steps you need to take along with saving money, because your dream is likely not just a financial one.

You may need to downsize your possessions. Additional training may be required. You may need to physically train for your goal. Perhaps you need partners, and if so you'll need time to recruit them. All these factors come into play when setting a deadline.

You recall our fancy cake baker, Samantha. She began mapping out her start date with some very specific questions. How much money did she need to invest in upgrading her kitchen and getting her inspection and certification? What supplies did she need to buy? How soon could she anticipate repaying her investment with revenue? After working out the numbers and the timeline, Samantha was able to open her specialty cake business in just 6 weeks. Imagine her shock to be doing what she dreamed of in such a short period of time – and all because she finally gave herself permission to look up the requirements!

Samantha had already been pursuing her love of cake decorating as a hobby, so she had a ready client base willing to pay her from day one. All along, the only thing standing in her way was not doing the basic research on how to make her dream come true. Your dream might be very much like hers, one you can start relatively quickly because of a lower cost or a ready base of customers willing to pay back your initial investment quickly. But if you don't map out a timeline for making it happen, it simply won't.

Avoid Letting Others Dictate Your Date

You can also take into account the people close to you and needs they may have, but be very careful here. There will never – we repeat never – be a good time for you to change your life when the people around you want you to stay the same. If you leave the deadline up to them, it just won't happen. So, definitely consider delaying the start of your dream a month or so for your daughter's high school graduation or your sister's surgery, but do not put off your dream for the "fuzzy" kind of "she needs me" or "what will he/she do" when I'm busy traveling / inventing / writing / building a business kind of scenarios.

Trust us on this. People can get along fine – and sometimes better – without your intervention into their problems. I found this out the hard way when I first moved away from my family over 10 years ago. I had been Ms. Bossy Pants for quite some time, giving my opinion on everything and getting involved with every minor crisis in my family members' lives. I found it gratifying – and humbling – to see them carry on just fine without my interference, living happy, healthy lives. It made me realize I should have been focusing on my own life all along.

If you want to know the exact details as to how we came up with our date, keep reading. (If this level of detail is too much, just skip down to the next subheading and start working on your own. We don't mind.)

The timeline for us was based on a couple of things: annual work bonuses and 40th birthdays. We started amassing our dream cash at age 37 with a goal of traveling around the world the year we both turned 40. That gave us just over two years to reach our goal of $75,000 (two years of travel at $36,500/year).

We added in our current savings of $10,000 to start, so we had $65,000 to save in 25 months. Basic math showed us we needed to save $2600 US per month. We further adjusted that monthly savings by deducting expected yearly bonuses from work for those two years plus our income tax returns to come up with our final savings number. We planned to leave on our trip just after the second bonus came in from work, on October 1, 2010.

When do you want to reach your financial goal for your dream?

You might be feeling overwhelmed at the idea of setting a date right now. You may even be discounting our methods because we had a much bigger or much smaller budget than yours. That's okay. Because what we're going to reveal next will convince you.

Once we put our time and attention toward our goal, it came at us faster than we ever imagined. Once we started saving, we saw the world in a whole new light, and we came up with other ways of making money – ways we'll share with you in the coming chapters – that helped us reach our goal in far less time than we estimated.

These plans have a way of speeding up when you put the full force of your attention to them. You're powerful in ways you cannot even imagine, and taking steps right now toward your goal – even if it is projected 5 years in the future – will start paying dividends to you almost immediately. And we wouldn't be surprised if you reached your goal in record time. We sure did. But you won't know if you don't start.

How to Set the Date

To come up with your deadline, you only need to combine your expectations with some simple math.

- To amass $12,000 in one year, you need to put back $1,000 per month.

- To save it in two years, you need to put back $500 per month.
- To save it in three years, you need to put back $333.33 per month.

You can see how this works, right? If you're expecting lump sums of money, like tax returns, gifts/inheritances, or bonuses from work, you can add this to the calculation as well. Add in any existing savings you want to use. Are you going to sell something to generate cash (or a lot of somethings)? Add in your projected revenue to your goal. (We'll talk about side jobs and extra income in Chapter 13).

Cash Goal: $12,000

- 1 Year Plan = $1,000/month
- 2 Year Plan = $500/month
- 3 Year Plan = $333.33/month

Now let's add in the logistical pieces to your dream:

- Do you require any training or certifications? If so, how long will it take?
- Do you need the help of other people/companies to make it happen? How does this affect your timeline?
- Are there any big events you need to work around (keeping in mind there will never be a clear time)?

If you used Mint, SmartyPig, or MoneyDashboard to help you estimate your savings goals before, you can fiddle with the numbers in their online calculators to help you determine a deadline that is reasonable for you.

Keep adjusting until you come up with a timeline and a monthly savings goal that is aggressive but doable. It gets much easier as you go, and in the coming chapters we'll show you how to add to add extra money to your goal every month to speed up your timeline.

Once you come up with your deadline, write it on your bathroom mirror, put it in your datebook, or whatever you need to do to see it every single day. This is your new Independence Day, and you're going to start working toward it right now.

Chapter Summary

Setting the date for your dream is like taking your first step off the starting line when the whistle blows. You have a finish line in front of you and you are estimating how long it will take you to run the race. It is the one piece of motivation with urgency, and once you set a date, the clock starts ticking.

There are some considerations in setting a deadline, mainly how long it will take you to save the sum of money needed to finance your dream. But there are other considerations, too, such as training, education, and gathering resources or partners to make your dream come true. Another outside factor is the reaction of friends and family. Not all of them will be thrilled with your decisions, and some may throw up roadblocks to delay your start. Some of these considerations are real and should be analyzed, but most are not. Until you give yourself permission to live the life of your dreams, you run the risk of others controlling your destiny.

We're now at the end of the Dream section of this book. By now you have:

- Clarified the dream in your mind
- Aligned it with your mate (if you have one)
- Created a sexy piece of Dream Porn to stay motivated
- Priced out your dream, and

- Set a date.

Are you feeling pretty good about things? The next section will be far more hands-on as we create the systems and habits that will build your nest egg and put you well on your way to living your dream.

Section II: Save

this covers it all, from gifts to tax returns to work bonuses and even selling your junk

Chapter 7: Secure Your Vault

"If you cannot make money from one dollar--if you do not coax one dollar to work hard for you, you won't know how to make money out of one thousand dollars."

~E. S. Kinnear

Before you accumulate the first cent for your dream, you need a secure place to keep it. And by "secure" we mostly mean secure from *you*. If you haven't ever saved a substantial amount of money before, it will be very tempting to use your growing dream fund for emergencies (we're going to create a separate budget item for those) and not-so-emergencies (concert tickets, a weekend trip, or that great pair of boots). Actually setting up the account is simple, but we're going to cover the hands-off nature of this account in detail to stress how important it is that you guard it from yourself.

Regular people might call it a savings account, but we have dubbed it The Vault for a very simple reason. Once your money goes in, it does not come out until you reach your goal. It is out of your reach. Picture your guard dog standing at attention in front of The Vault door, protecting you from yourself. Yep, he's guarding your money now. Are you getting the idea?

> *The Vault is the account where you will keep your money. It is a one-way street. You can't touch this. Money goes in, but it does not come out until you have hit your goal.*

The Vault is a one-way track from your start line to the finish line, and you only get to see the proceeds when you break through the ribbon. Erase from your mind the idea that there is any sort of withdrawal mechanism available. Once you deposit money in The Vault it becomes the property of Your Dream.

You might be thinking that you can just stash it in your regular savings account, the one you use for household repairs, emergency vet bills, and taxes. But you can't. That account is used to being a two-way street. You put money in when you can, and you take money out when you need it. We're all a little iffy on the concept of 'need' and can justify one to ourselves without too much effort. This is why you'll be putting your dream money somewhere else.

This account is different. It is *sacred*. You will never withdraw a cent until it is time to start living the dream. It has a different purpose than your regular savings account and should be completely separate from your day-to-day life. Just like you gave power to your dream by naming it in Chapter 4, you are going to give financial priority to your dream by separating this money from your living expenses.

It typically doesn't cost anything to set up a savings account at your bank, brokerage firm, or credit union, and in fact they will probably pay you a bit of interest to hold your money. One we particularly like is Smarty Pig (in the US and Australia) because it is focused on achieving dreams just like yours.

Matt learned the importance of setting up a separate account for his family's dream of a sabbatical in Indonesia. You'll remember Matt and his family were not on the same page about the dream, and he got caught up more in the idea of doing it than actually making it happen. One of his mistakes was not creating a separate account for the Dream savings. When unexpected expenses cropped up, he took the money to pay for them out of his regular savings account. The account was not special, and it was not earmarked exclusively for the Dream. He paid dental bills out of the same account that was housing his dream money. It's no wonder it stopped feeling special and he fell off the wagon. When his family recommitted to the goal later, they separated this money out and created a Vault, and it is no small coincidence they reached their goal when they started taking it seriously.

How We Set Up Our Vault

We set up our Vault at a very precarious time in the economy, and that informed our decision as to how to do it. We decided to take this trip around the world on September 1, 2008. If you live in the US, you might recall that this is when several of the big banks started failing and the growing financial crisis hit full on. Markets outside the US were impacted in the coming months, and the entire world saw an economic shadow that is still impacting many countries as we write this book.

The markets were in freefall and very unpredictable, and we were scared of putting our money there. We had already seen our retirement accounts lose money, and we didn't want the same thing to happen to our dream money. (We have much more time to let the retirement accounts recover than we do our dream money.) The money market account we chose gave us only 1.5% interest, but since our goal was to keep the money we saved and not maximize returns, this was okay. Remember, this is your dream money, something you want fairly quickly and without drama.

(Remember when we said there was never a perfect time to follow your dream? This would be an excellent example of that.)

We happened to be in New York City on the day Lehman Brothers went under. We sat in a little park near Wall Street next to all the camera crew vans who were there to film, we asked each other if we were crazy to think about doing this when the world was falling apart. We still couldn't think of a good reason not to. In fact, it was starting to sound like the most logical thing in the world when all the other "rules" around us were being broken. That's the funny thing about dreams; when you finally decide to go for them, hardly anything can deter you from your decision.

We opened up a money market account at E-Trade to house our Vault. We then set up a direct deposit from work for our basic savings payment each month. We never saw this money, never had a chance to spend it, and kept ourselves far, far away from it. (If your company offers direct deposit you can usually have it filtered into more than one account by specific amounts or percentages, so don't worry that you have to put all of your paycheck into one account or another.)

As time went on and we paid things off or made other changes to our spending that freed up more money, we set up automatic transfers to The Vault from our regular checking account. This is why it's so important to have this functionality in all your accounts. You will not want to go to your HR department at work and change your direct deposit info every month as you free up expenses.

We paid off the car and that $350 monthly payment to Volkswagen became a payment to The Vault via automatic transfer. When we cut out the cable bill, downsized our cell phone plans, and negotiated lower insurance premiums, those payments became automatic transfers to The Vault. It didn't take long before we had a significant automatic transfer from our checking account each month *in addition* to the money we had already earmarked for direct deposit from our paychecks.

When we sold something on Craigslist, we immediately transferred the money to The Vault. When we did something that saved us money, like Warren cutting his own hair, we transferred the money we would have spent to The Vault. When we made money from our side jobs, it went into The Vault. It reinforced in our minds there was an end goal in mind and we were regularly working toward our dream. Over time, we started looking forward to doing the activities that led to these transfers.

Willpower is not the answer

But we weren't perfect in our savings plan, which is why we're going to talk about the importance of automation. Your good intentions and willpower aren't enough because at the end of the day, you're still just a regular human being like the rest of us (we'll talk more about willpower in Chapter 10). There will be times when you want to spend the money earmarked for your dream on something more immediate. And if the cash is in your hand and the immediate gratification is right in front of you, it will be damn hard to say no. This is why automation is so important and why we advocate setting up these habits from the start. It's like muscle memory for athletes: regular practice means you will know what to do when the game is on.

When you're weak – and you will be sometimes – automation will shore up your defenses.

Only a masochist would work on building up willpower. Who wants to deprive themselves of something they really want just to say they did it? Not us, and probably not you.

Don't leave it to yourself and willpower to make your payments to The Vault. There's no reason to test your willpower just for the hell of it. If you can take this temptation away, do it. Take advantage of the resources out there to help you stay on track. When your mind starts realizing that this monthly savings plan is a set thing and not something you can do anything about – like train schedules, meetings with your boss, and the fact that you'll have a birthday every year – you'll find it much easier to manage. Leave it up to yourself every month to make those payments and you will fight with your alter ego every 30 days. And you do not want to battle that guy. He's a smooth talker!

Remember that this dream is the desire of your higher self, the one who wants to live an extraordinary life, and you'll constantly be doing battle with your lower self who simply wants immediate gratification. You have to say "no" to fleeting desires to be able to say "yes" to the important ones.

The Roadmap (which is the budget we'll create in Chapter 12) is the path to get you to your Dream, but the Vault is the vehicle that will drive you there. Make sure you fuel up regularly.

Important points about setting up your Vault

- Once you determine your savings amount each payday, you can set up a direct deposit to go directly into The Vault. This is the best way because it means you never even touch that money, giving you zero chance to find another purpose for it.

- For "found money" (we'll cover that in Chapter 13) and other extras that may come your way, you should have access to transfer money from your checking account into The Vault. Your banking institution will tell you that this transfer works both ways, but you will erase that little tidbit from your mind immediately after setting up the account. Money only goes in.

- Once you set it up, you can add the account details to your Mint.com (US/Canada) or MoneyDashboard (UK) account or your personal budget software (more on that later). Here you'll be able to track your savings and see the funding for your dream grow.

Chapter Summary

It is important to set your dream money aside from your day-to-day spending. When your dream fund is mingled with your everyday spending, it quickly becomes less special. Over time, it becomes nonexistent. It's hard not to spend the money when it is mixed in with the grocery money and the entertainment budget, and it is difficult to appreciate how your savings are building up if you can't easily track it.

Putting your dream money into The Vault solves this problem. This separate account allows you to keep your dream separate from your everyday life. It also allows you to set up automatic deposits from your paycheck so you never even have to be tempted to spend the money. Why test your willpower if you don't have to?

Automating your savings also means easily tracking deposits and spending with online financial tools like Mint.com, MoneyDashboard.com, or your own personal software. When you make it easy to save and track money, you are more likely to continue doing it. Don't overcomplicate things.

In the next chapter you'll analyze your current spending and put it together in a budget. We'll call this the Roadmap, though it will hardly look like a path to your dream when you first see it. Keep in mind we're just getting started here, and to do that we need to have an accurate picture of where you are right now. If you want to work ahead, start gathering your credit card and bank statements along with your other bills right now.

Chapter 8: Calculate Current Spending

"Too many people spend money they haven't earned, to buy things they don't want, to impress people they don't like."

~Will Rogers

How much cash do you have on you right now? No peeking, just say it out loud right now. Now check your wallet or your purse and count it. Were you close or completely off the mark? You can try the same thing with your checking or savings account balance. Do you know it or do you have to log in to look it up?

How about your groceries – do you know what you spend each month on average? Or what you spend on fuel every year for your car? How about your clothes or medical expenses? Movies and popcorn? Takeout pizza?

These may sound like little things, or things you *have* to have anyway. No sense in keeping track of that, right? Well, it's that kind of thinking that will keep you exactly where you are right now. You are leaking money from your dream when you don't monitor your daily spending.

It's your money, and you should know how much you have and how much you're spending.

If you don't, it will be almost impossible for you to save the money you need to fund your dream.

We found out the hard way that we were spending a huge percentage of our savings goal every single month on eating out. To top it off, we were getting fat in the process, a definite no-win situation. Does the following story sound familiar?

Dinner was a delivery from our favorite Chinese restaurant, and we were chomping on Crab Rangoon and Kung Pao chicken as we worked through the budget one night after work. Putting the numbers in the boxes so we could start cutting expenses was part of the deal to save money, and even though we weren't looking forward to it, we knew we could cut a little here and a little there.

Warren looked up from his computer with wide eyes. "You'd better come look at this."

Warren entered all of our expenses from the previous month – credit card charges, cash outlay, checks – as well as the annualized expenses for things like insurance. After popping in our income, we should have had a nice shiny budget to work out a saving plan.

It sounds crazy to write this now, but I actually thought he was going to show me a chunk of money previously unaccounted for, something we could use to save for our trip without impacting our lifestyle too much. I was still feeling giddy from making the decision to travel full-time, and I had the feeling everything was just going to somehow work out. I popped another Crab Rangoon into my mouth and walked over.

What I saw was like a slap in the face. There was no way that was our budget, that we were spending that kind of money! He must have entered our mortgage twice or miscalculated something. How did the 'dining out' budget get to be so big? And how did we ever spend so much money at IKEA? We must have bought one of every single thing they sell.

We looked at the details in disbelief. $200 spent on morning coffee and donuts each month. Eating out an average of 13 times per week between the two of us. Filling up the cars was always a drag, but seeing the monthly totals brought tears to my eyes.

This is the point where we could have started laying blame on each other for overspending on this or that, but it was pretty obvious it was a shared problem. We chose to travel together, to buy things for the house together, and to eat out together.

The things we thought of as "no big deal" expenses were eating us alive, and we could easily visualize our savings plan by looking at those numbers. It was embarrassing and humbling to see how far our own actions had pushed us from the life we wanted to live, and it all came about through inattention.

When you don't know where your money is going, it will never go where you really want.

Our Chinese dinner lost all flavor, and we sat staring at each other as the food grew cold. We could either take this information and do something about it, or we could try to forget it and go back to the life we had. I won't kid you that this was a quick decision, because it would have been easy to just hide our heads back in the sand. But after looking at the numbers, it was hard to choose takeout food, donuts, and cheap home furnishings over the thing we most wanted in the world. When you look at it that way, the decision is easy.

It was our last Chinese food until we were actually in China 4 years later. I'll take the real thing over takeout any day.

In order for you to save money, you're going to have to stop spending it somewhere – in fact, probably several somewheres. You may be shaking your head right now and telling me you can't squeeze blood from a stone, but I'm telling you that you often can.

The first step in finding the money for your dream is to know where you're currently spending it.

You may think you already know where your money goes, or that your online bank account is sufficient to show you where your money is going. You're wrong.

Don't skip this step. It's the basis from which everything else flows, and if you skip it you will never make the most of your money-saving efforts. You want to amass the most money in the shortest amount of time, and it all starts with knowing where you are right this second. You can't effectively move ahead if you don't know where you are to start.

Brenda knew her spending was putting her deeper into debt and further away from her dream of living and teaching overseas. And living in expensive New York City certainly wasn't helping things. When she analyzed where she spent her disposable income, it came down to 2 big categories: eating out and buying shoes. As much as she loved the dining choices in NYC and the feel of great shoes on her feet, she knew she'd have to reduce both if she wanted to make her dream come true. She brown-bagged her lunch every single day for 2 years, and she only replaced shoes as they wore out. It was a big change from her former life, but over the course of 2 years she paid down her credit card debt enough to take a lower-paying teaching job in Brazil, the first stop in her plan to teach around the world. Now she wears flip-flops and sandals every day and eats out 3 times a week.

Calculating Your Monthly Spending

We could go old school here and give you a spreadsheet to input all your financial info, show you how to analyze with a bunch of formulas, and then do some serious number-crunching judo with a #2 pencil. But we like the modern conveniences, so this is where we call in our friends (and soon to be yours, too) Mint.com and MoneyDashboard.

Both of these services (Mint for the US and Canada and MoneyDashboard for the UK) pull all your financial information together into one place, giving you a simple dashboard to keep track of your savings and expenses at the drop of a hat. If your life is managed by your mobile phone, you can even use them on your Android or iPhone. We have used Mint.com for years, and we love how you can get an overall look at your financial picture in just a moment.

> *Note: Some people may be concerned about entering their personal usernames and passwords on the Mint or MoneyDashboard sites to get the dashboard. We have used Mint for years without a problem, but if that is a concern to you there are software packages that allow you to track your money on your own computer, like Quicken (www.quicken.intuit.com). (Both Quicken and Mint are owned by Intuit.) Be sure to read and understand the security policies and procedures in any financial dashboard service you choose. And you can always use the budget spreadsheet we have created for you at: www.dreamsavedo.com/#resources*

You can use these free services to track your Vault, your spending, and even to create the Roadmap budget you will use to amass the cash for your big dream. It will make the whole process easier, and the easier it is, the more likely you will do it. Another bonus is that both services are free.

> *The Roadmap* is the ever-evolving budget
> you will use to find and track the money for
> your Dream. Use yours, Mint's or
> MoneyDashboard's or even a piece of paper in
> a notebook. We don't care. Just make one.

The hardest work in creating the Roadmap is in gathering your financial information the first time. Before you start, gather it all together. If you don't, it will be really easy to overlook something as you go.

- Credit card statements
- Bank statements
- Utilities
- Rent/Mortgage
- Insurance (health, home, life, auto)
- Monthly record of all cash spent (you can track this in a small notebook)
- Paycheck stubs
- Gifts (holidays, birthdays, etc.)
- Charitable donations
- Medical bills
- Tax returns
- Other income receipts

In short, you should have a record of every cent that you spent the previous month plus all your sources of income. Don't forget fixed expenses like insurance that may only get billed once or twice a year.

Calculating Variable Expenses

The same goes for things like gifts and a small "emergency fund" you can calculate based on your last year's expenses (medical emergencies, car repair, home repair, etc.). Do not forget to add these in, because if you don't it will wreak havoc on your budget when – not if – they happen. If you did not calculate these last year, it's not a problem. Scan your credit card receipts, calendar, or bank balance from last year to remind yourself of what you spent when you were not expecting it.

Speaking of credit card spending, this is where it is important to get specific. Instead of just listing your credit card minimum payment as an expense, you'll need to break out your spending and categorize it. You'll need to do the same with your daily cash spending (if you're still quaint like us and use real money). This is the only way you'll get an accurate picture of where your money is really going. It will do you no good to list $250/month as "credit card" if you don't know where that money is going. It may be an unavoidable expense like car repair or it may be $250 worth of lamps at IKEA. You have to spell it out so you'll know and so you can make wise decisions on that kind of spending in the future.

Your category breakdowns should be specific enough to help you refine your budget but not so extreme you won't keep up with it. For instance, we separate out grocery store spending and eating out because we know we have a tendency to go overboard on eating out. If we lump-summed it into a category called Food it would be harder to track and adjust.

The same holds true for your vehicle (maintenance vs. fuel vs. insurance) and any large spending that falls into a subset of another, like buying expensive video games and lumping that into the "entertainment" budget you use for movie rentals and the occasional music download. If you think you might be spending too much on something, it's important not to hide it within a category so you don't have to face it.

Below is a sample list of categories; you can modify to fit your situation.

- Housing – shelter
- Pensions, Social Security
- Housing – utilities, fuels, public services
- Food – food at home
- Transportation – vehicle purchases
- Transportation – other expenses
- Healthcare
- Entertainment
- Food – food away from home
- Transportation – gasoline, motor oil
- Apparel and Services
- Cash Contributions (optional retirement and cash savings)
- Housing – household furnishings, equipment
- Education
- Housing – household operations
- Miscellaneous
- Housing – housekeeping supplies
- Alcoholic Beverages
- Personal Care
- Life, other personal insurance
- Reading

You can go through the process of entering it all into a spreadsheet now, or you can do the easy thing and link all your accounts to your Mint or MoneyDashboard account, quickly go through your expenses to make sure they are categorized correctly, and easily see what your current spending looks like. (And by that we mean "easy to visualize," not necessarily "easy to see." It might hurt a bit.)

Your First Roadmap (aka Budget)

This is very easy to create with an online financial service or personal budgeting software once you gather all the information. It's not that much harder to do it on paper or with an Excel spreadsheet.

- Gather all your current financial statements as well as year-end statements for the last couple of years.
- Document your cash spending for a month (or estimate to get started and revise after you track for a month).
- Average the yearly spending for each category and divide by 12 to get a monthly spending average. (This is important because you spend more on some things at different times of the year – like heat, gifts, lawn care, household repairs, medical expenses, and insurance.)
- Split out credit card spending by category.
- Insert your figures into your budget, aka The Roadmap (either on paper, using an online service like Mint.com, or in your own software).
- Don't forget all your sources of income: salary, tax returns, gifts, and bonuses.
- Look at the final balance.
- Pour yourself a stiff drink or reach for some chocolate.

Many people are shocked at this point to find out that they spend more than they make.

It seems like it would be easy to know this, but with the availability of credit and loans that's not always the case. You might be hyperaware of your monthly cash flow but not necessarily of your overall financial picture. It's important to know where all your money is located now. Make sure to list all your various accounts (money market, savings, checking, loans, mortgage, brokerage, etc.) List all your accounts and the current balances as well to understand your complete picture. When you know exactly where your money goes and how much time you have to work to purchase and maintain the things in your life, you will have a completely different perspective in your future spending. (We'll address your existing credit card debt in Chapter 9.)

If you're hyperventilating right now, don't worry. We're going to improve your breathing very soon by showing you how to streamline your spending and maximize your cash by revising this budget Roadmap into something that will guide you toward your dream. It may seem painful to go through this process, but the first step toward success is simply knowing your starting line.

Chapter Summary

You might be hyperaware of your monthly cash flow, but most people are not monitoring their overall financial situation every month (or even every year). In fact, a review of your spending might show you a significant chunk of the money you want to save being spent in just one or two specific areas.

When you break it down by category, combining all your cash, debit, and credit spending together to get a total number, you might be surprised at how much of your income goes to eating out, entertainment, clothes, or even sodas (at my peak, I was drinking 5 Diet Cokes per day, spending $1,825 per year).

When you calculate your spending, don't forget to account for irregular or seasonal expenses like heating, repairs, insurance, taxes, or even gifts and holidays (more on that in Chapter 11). You may not always be able to plan when the car will need maintenance, but you can plan that it eventually will and have some funds set aside for it in your budget.

Now that you have your existing budget in front of you, you can start working to turn it into the Roadmap to your dream. Since no one's dream includes credit card debt, we'll start working on this in the next chapter.

Chapter 9: Eliminate Credit Card Debt

"Credit buying is much like being drunk. The buzz happens immediately and gives you a lift... The hangover comes the day after."

- Joyce Brothers, PhD

The average credit card debt in a US household is $15,418. How would you like to have that cash for your dream fund? If you live in the UK, the average consumer debt of your fellow citizens sits at £5,934. The Reserve Bank of Australia reports credit card debt has grown 30% over the past 5 years, currently sitting at an average of $3333 *per card.* No doubt, the world has a problem with plastic.

Warren and I both came into our relationship with debt. As divorced 30-somethings, we had the financial baggage of our former relationships plus the debt we incurred individually as we created new lives for ourselves. It never occurred to us not to buy the things we wanted because we had the means to do so – well, at least we had the credit to do so.

Shortly after we married and decided to combine our finances, we woke up and said, "enough." Having watched my parents struggle with debt after my father was laid off and worrying over our own budget while

Warren was between jobs for a few months, we knew it was a gamble to simply live paycheck to paycheck. This is when we started the serious work of paying off our debt, which we'll detail below.

But enough about us; let's talk about you. This book is about dreaming, saving, and doing to live your dream. But no amount of savings is going to get you closer to your dream while you have credit card debt hanging over your head. If you aren't paying off your balance in full every single month and avoiding all finance charges, you're not in control of your credit cards. They're in control of you.

Oh sure, it starts out as a lovely relationship. "Only for emergencies," you say, or maybe "just to build my credit." You use it to buy gas when you don't have enough in the bank to fill your tank. While you're there, you add on a car wash and a soda. Then it becomes buying the clothes or nice dinners out or electronic gadgets that you could save up for but you want right now. And before long it becomes gifts you can't afford and even the occasional cash advance to last you until the next payday. When you start taking a cash advance from one credit card to make the minimum payment on the other, you've reached rock bottom. Even if you're using your cards to get mileage bonuses and other perks but still paying finance charges every month along with your minimum payment, you're losing money.

You may not be using your credit cards wisely, but what can you expect when you never learned how? Getting a credit card when you have no savings or money management experience is a recipe for disaster, and most people get their first credit cards before they have enough sense to come in out of the rain. They mess up early and often stay that way for years and years because they don't know how to stop. *(Or was that just us?)*

If you have credit card debt right now, there is no reason to continue beating yourself up. This book is all about living in the present and working toward a better future, so we will not be dwelling on the mistakes of the past. You did it, and now you have to fix it – simple as that.

There is no dream we can imagine that includes credit card debt, so let's get to work on eliminating yours.

Learn how to pay off your credit card debt

We could write another book just on this subject. When we started saving for our trip around the world we were already out of debt after working for several years to pay off credit cards from our previous divorces and overspending habits.

We have some fun stories about how we got into debt (oh, that first year after the divorce!). But since we're focusing on amassing the cash for your dream, we're going to briefly talk about consumer debt reduction and let you dive into the recommended resources at the end of the guide if you need targeted help with this.

The Basics of Debt Reduction

- **Pay more than the minimum payment.** If you only ever make the minimum payment, you will never pay off your debt. Credit card companies count on this because they depend on the interest.

- **Stop incurring new debt.** Easier said than done, right? This is why we recommend leaving your credit cards at home. Carry your cash and debit cards with you, and if an emergency happens you can always use what you have on hand to at least get back home to get your credit cards. But you'll find it rarely comes to that, and the temptations you have to spend will be stopped by not having the ability to do it. (We'll talk more in Chapter 10 about the fallacy of willpower and how to bypass it. Don't test it if you don't have to.)

- **Spend less than you make.** You may have already discovered you are spending more than your annual income each year, and learning how to live within your means is a valuable life lesson in more ways than one. It teaches you to value what's really important, learn the difference between need and want, and evaluate the level of work required for the outcomes you desire. We'll be covering ideas for generating additional income in Chapter 13, which will help you get out of the hole you're in and build your dream. We want you to learn to live within your means so your life is always your own. When you owe someone else, you are never truly free to do what you want.

The debt snowball

Many personal finance experts recommend the Debt Snowball strategy. Pick one debt to pay off at a time, maintaining just a minimum payment on everything else while you load up everything you can against this one debt. It's a psychological boost because you can more quickly see the debt reducing than you can when you pay just a little bit more across the board on all your debt, and the feeling of accomplishment when you do pay it off spurs you to snowball your next bit of debt. You just keep going until all your debt is gone.

Some people do this in a logical fashion with the highest-interest debt first, but others have found success by focusing on the lowest total amount of debt first. This is also a psychological boost because you're eliminating entire bills, even if your debt is still high. Imagine how much better you'd feel if your mail dropped off to just grocery store fliers and the occasional card from a friend?

Strategies for Managing Debt

Most people don't realize they can call their credit card company and ask for assistance. The same works for the bank holding your car or house loan. When you're in a bind, a month's reprieve on a payment or a slight reduction in an interest rate can give you the breathing room to make your way forward.

Remember, these offers of help always come with a price tag. Always research the consequences of these actions (and get it in writing) so you can decide if it is really worth it to you. We've outlined some of them below along with the caveats from our personal experience. Some strategies for managing debt:

- **Transfer balances from high-interest cards** to lower-interest cards. You can do this with your existing cards if you have available credit on a lower-interest card. You can also take advantage of 6-month "introductory" programs on new cards and transfer a high-interest balance over. Read the fine print to make sure you won't incur a fee for transferring at the end of the introductory period (some credit cards will retroactively apply their normal interest rate when you do) or that the new rate applies to the entire balance you transfer and not just a portion of it. The other downside to this is you may accumulate too much open credit in the form off all these cards, which is very tempting and can hurt your credit score overall. It's also really easy to forget to change your card over before the new rate hits, so we'd recommend paying very close attention and putting reminders on your calendar. If you go this route, make sure you understand the terms and conditions completely.

- **Skip a loan payment** (and adding it – and the additional interest – onto the end of the loan). This can come in handy when you're dealing with a temporary gap in income or a large emergency expense. My car finance company allowed this twice during the length of the loan, and it was a handy option for me when I changed jobs and had to wait an additional month for my first paycheck. My 1.9% interest rate on the car loan was far lower than my credit card, so it made sense to delay the car payment rather than charge the payment. Again, make sure you understand all the terms and conditions in this plan. It isn't such a great deal if you have a high interest loan and a low-interest credit card.

- **Renegotiate bank fees and terms**. It's harder to do this when you're the one needing the favor, so we recommend doing this in a non-emergency situation if possible. Call your bank and ask them to remove your annual fee and/or ask for a lower percentage rate or repayment schedule on your credit card. Do your homework first and know your options. It is cheaper for a company to retain an existing client than recruit a new one, so most are open to working with you if you have a history of making your payments on time and negotiate in a reasonable and calm manner.

Check out Ramit Sethi's website, www.IWillTeachYouToBeRich.com for excellent scripts on how to negotiate rates with your bank.

- **Debt management programs** will help you negotiate your rates and come up with a workable solution to pay off your debt. While this seems like a great solution, there are some big warnings to heed. I used this program to pay off $16,000 in debt, and I did not understand at the start that it would negatively impact my credit score. Because these companies negotiate new interest rates for your debt, credit card companies consider it much like a charge off because they are not getting the full interest (a charge off is a declaration that a debt is unlikely to be paid in full or on time; this gives the credit card company a tax exemption). I paid off the debt at a reduced interest rate, but my credit was dinged for the next 5 years. If you can negotiate rates on your own and discipline yourself to pay off your debt it is better in the long run.

- **Borrow against your assets**. Do you have a life insurance policy with cash value or own your home? You can borrow against these assets (essentially borrowing money from yourself) at a lower interest rate than your credit cards. But paying off debt instantly is a danger zone because you don't have the time to learn the lessons of responsibly using your credit cards. The potential pitfall here is taking out the loans, paying off your credit card debt, and then racking it up again. Then you're stuck with credit card debt and a loan payment. If you don't have the discipline to avoid this, don't go down this path.

- **Use your savings to pay off debt**. I know it sounds crazy since we're talking about big savings plans for your dream, but if you have several hundred or several thousand dollars in the bank drawing 1% interest and an equal or greater amount of credit card debt at 15%, it's foolish to keep paying money on your debt. Pay it off and start at zero for your dream; it will build up fast if you don't have to make credit card payments with interest at the same time. Be sure to leave a small amount in your savings for emergencies so you don't have to rely on your credit cards again.

Redefine Emergency

You probably need to redefine your definition of an emergency. We have covered the need for budgeting for household, automotive, and health emergencies already, and this cash should take the place of most situations in which you would normally use your credit card. If you "need" the card for something else – to keep yourself in all the creature comforts before next payday, to go out with your friends when cash is low, or to finance a lifestyle that is really outside your income level, then you may need to reevaluate your relationship with your credit card, because you're not the one in control anymore.

How Debt Fits into Your Dream

The short answer is that it doesn't. You don't want to be living the life of your dreams on borrowed money because there is always the downside of having to pay it back - with interest. But for the sake of the Roadmap budget, we need to account for your debt payoff. The first plan of attack is to reduce your debt where possible through negotiation with your bank, paying it off from savings or loans against your assets, or transferring balances. Once you've done that, determine how you'll work off your remaining debt balance using the debt snowball. You can adjust the credit card debt line item on your budget as you gradually pay off these debts.

We'll be showing you how to free up money and add income in the subsequent chapters, and these strategies will also help you pay down your debt so you can live your dream.

Our final word on credit card debt:

Stop using your credit card *today*. Put it in a tray of water and stick it in the freezer. You won't be able to grab it and use it on a whim, but it will still be available in case of an emergency. If you think you cannot live without one in today's society, check out Smarty Pig's Cash Rewards Card, which is linked to your own bank account and earns you up to 10% back while spending your own money. No finance charges, no monthly statements. Just reload it when your balance gets low. This will help retrain your thinking on how to use a credit card.

Please realize that every time you use your credit card without the ability to pay it off when the bill comes due you're pushing yourself further and further away from the freedom you need to pursue your dream.

Debt and obligation are two different words for the same thing. The only thing you want to be obligated to is your dream.

Credit Card Debt Reduction Resources:

- Check out the following personal finance blogs who frequently write about consumer debt elimination strategies:
  - www.Fool.com
  - www.ManvsDebt.com
  - www.TheSimpleDollar.com
  - www.GetRichSlowly.org
- Mint, MoneyDashboard and Smarty Pig all have online tools to help create your credit card payoff plan. Set up goals around your specific credit card debt by using their handy tutorials.
- Become a savvier credit card consumer by negotiating better interest rates on your remaining debt. Learn some great strategies from money guru Ramit Sethi at: www.IWillTeachYouToBeRich.com/how-to-negotiate.

Chapter Summary

No matter what your dream, it doesn't include debt or worry about the ability to pay your bills every month. When you owe other people, it is hard to make yourself and your dreams a priority.

You can start the journey to a debt-free life with one simple step today: stop using your credit card for purchases you cannot pay off at the end of the month. Make it a practice to use your credit card like a debit card – or better yet, just use a debit card – so you are constantly drawing from an available pool of money instead of digging a hole of debt.

In your everyday life, this can be as easy as leaving your credit card at home so even when temptation strikes, you can't do anything about it. If a true emergency arises and you don't have the cash to pay for it, you can easily retrieve your card from home.

Once you've stopped the bleeding of cash from credit card spending, it's time to address the debt you've already accumulated. You can do this in a couple of ways: 1) Pay off your highest-interest debts first, or 2) Use the Debt Snowball method of paying off the smallest amounts first to give yourself a psychological incentive. Either way is fine; just pick one that works for you.

Another effective strategy is to list your debts on paper along with amounts, interest rates, and terms along with a contact number. Many times you can negotiate better rates and payback options by simply asking. You can also transfer higher-interest loans into a lower-interest credit card or a home equity line of credit, though you need to read the fine print to make sure it works for you long term.

When you resolve to live without debt, you'll have more options available to you in living your dream. You may not always have the latest electronics or buy new shoes every week, but you will have the freedom to pretty much come and go as you like, and there is no possession on earth more valuable than controlling your time.

In the next chapter, we'll give you a simple phrase to use when the temptation to spend strikes. You're going to like this one.

Chapter 10: Create Your Phrase to Save

"A bargain ain't a bargain unless it's something you need."

~Sidney Carroll

With a $75,000 goal in mind and 25 months to reach it, we knew we had some pretty serious cuts to make in our spending. The more we thought about that number, the "numb"er we felt.

How do you wrap your head around a number that big when you're thinking about your daily expenses? Is my $20 savings at the grocery store really going to impact a number that big? It doesn't seem likely. And because of that disconnect it was hard to see how our daily activities impacted our long-term dream. It wasn't until we made the connection about comparing what we wanted to do on a day in our dream life to what we were currently spending that it finally clicked.

We were walking in our neighborhood when I spotted a gorgeous necklace in a shop window. I'm not much of a fine jewelry kinda gal, but I go weak in the knees at an original creation by an artist I can meet, someone who makes funky art you can wear. This gorgeous piece of personality and bold statement was $100, and I wanted it. As I pressed my face to the glass like a little kid at a toy store, Warren said the words that would lead our saving efforts from that day forward.

"Is that more important to you than a day on the road? Because it costs the same."

BINGO!

What a brilliant concept in such a simple statement. By focusing our saving efforts on a small but easily visualized segment of our overall figure, I could easily admire that necklace from the street and leave it in the store for someone else.

We estimated our dream life would cost $100/day, and instead of saving the full amount – $75,000 – we focused on $100 goals. We were finally able to see how our daily saving and spending connected with our overall goal. This concept became known as our **Phrase to Save**, and we used it every single day until we reached our goal.

At first we kept our little Phrase to Save to ourselves, gently chiding each other when we wanted to buy something inappropriate or high-fiving each other when we saved enough for a day or two of travel.

"Hey, that's 1.5 days on the road!" or "We just purchased ourselves a full afternoon on a trip around the world!"

Each payday we would celebrate our "days on the road" number going into savings instead of comparing how far away we were from the end goal. Imagining The Vault was holding the 'number of days on the road' made the process more encouraging than it ever would have been just slogging our way to the final number.

As time went by, our Phrase to Save occasionally slipped out in front of others. What started as a little mental trick between the two of us soon became the catchphrase in our circle of friends. They cheered us on as we accumulated 'days on the road' by saving money here and there in their presence. And when we chose to spend money, they could quickly calculate how many days on the road we were giving up by doing so.

Even now, well into our travels, we can't help but think about how many days of travel we're giving up to make any purchase outside our daily living expenses. Obviously we do sometimes, but we love it that this mantra still helps us stay on track and remember why we saved all this money in the first place.

Mental Judo

If you aren't freaking out a little bit right now at the prospect of reaching your number by your deadline, then you're made of stronger stuff than us. You've set the bar pretty high by stating The Dream, designing your Dream Porn, Pricing it out and Setting the Date. You've secured The Vault and also created a plan for your credit card debt. Now we're going to suggest you lower the bar to get there.

Sounds counterintuitive, doesn't it? We can explain.

It is exciting to embark on something new, especially that first day, week or month. You still have the bright beacon of the end result in front of you, and even your biggest temptations won't sway you from your goal. But as time goes by, the day to day of life creeps in. It's harder to imagine your big dream when you have a stressful project at work, an unexpected expense crops up, or you just feel exhausted at the end of the week and want to fall back into the comfort of old routines.

Your motivation and willpower are not foolproof, so we're going to strengthen them with some mental judo.

In all things, we look for the easiest path to change because it is the one most likely to stick for the long term.

Chip and Dan Heath recommend you set the bar so low you can *step* over it in their book, *Switch: How to Change Things When Change is Hard*. They call this "motivating the elephant" (the emotional mind), which is generally reluctant to move. It takes small change, easier goals, and a head start to inspire the elephant to move. In fact, you may recognize the "head start" at work in the Debt Snowball we discussed in Chapter 9. By seeing your total number of debts decrease, even if you are paying off the smallest debts first, you are motivated to keep at it. It's a small shift in thinking that creates a huge impact in your long-term motivation and success.

The time to combat these temptations is before they start, when your enthusiasm is at an all-time high. You do this in part through automation, like the direct deposit you set up for your payments into The Vault and the financial management site you chose to keep track of your money. The rest of your temptations you'll have to *life hack* a bit with new habits, and we're going to show you how. (The term *life hack* refers to anything that solves an everyday problem in a clever or non-obvious way.)

Stanford researcher BJ Fogg, PhD, also advocates baby steps when it comes to long-term change. His popular website Tiny Habits highlights the 3 ways change can happen: through an epiphany, changing your context, and taking baby steps. You may have already had your epiphany, the event that led to you buying this book in the first place. Now we're going to focus on changing your context (the way you see the things around you) and taking those baby steps. So let's start where you're going to need it the most: in your spending and saving.

You see, focusing on that big number is just going to freak you out. If it doesn't freak you out, it's going to seem so unattainable that it won't feel real. And if it doesn't feel real, it won't be long before you're veering off The Roadmap, your goal banished to dream purgatory to finish out its life sad, lonely, and unfulfilled. You don't want that to happen.

The plan you're formulating today seems workable, livable and doable. But we're telling you weeks from now, months in, a year in, you're going to need a little help to keep going. We want you to be successful, and we aren't making up these ideas just to fill space on a page. We actually did every single one of these, even the ones that might seem a little corny to you right now. One of the most powerful is the Phrase to Save, the very one we created that day at the jewelry store window.

Create Your Phrase to Save

> The **Phrase to Save** is the mantra you will
> develop to keep you on track with your daily
> spending and celebrate your savings.

Remember, the Phrase to Save isn't there to keep you from spending money; it's there to remind you why you chose to save in the first place and whether this option in front of you fits in with that dream. It's there to "change your context" as Dr. Fogg suggested, and it's in a small enough figure to be considered a baby step, at least when compared to your overall goal.

Our goal was pretty easy to break down into a bite-sized chunk we could relate to in our daily spending. One day of travel was $100, and every $100 in the bank was a day on the road. Both saving and spending were easier with this figure in mind instead of the overall $75,000.

To set up your own Phrase to Save, you need only think about a component of your dream, something you can easily visualize. It can be a 'day in the life' figure like ours, or it can be something concrete you need to purchase for your dream (building material for your new house, wheels for your new car, hours of learning for your education, or pages written for your new novel). Think back to when you priced your dream and how you did your research. The key is to break the number down into small, bite-sized chunks you can use every day to compare spending and keep you on track.

Our Phrase to Save: "Do I want this more than I want a day on the road?

Get creative, keeping in mind the visual has to be something easy to see and something you really want. For us, the idea of buying $100 worth of clothes – clothes we wouldn't even wear on our travels – was ridiculous in comparison to a day of exploring the world. It was fast, easy, and powerful, and that's what you should aim for in your Phrase to Save.

Matt and his family took it a step further by creating a Phrase to Save box. They decorated it with pictures of their dream – images of Indonesia and time spent together as a family – and used it to monitor their spending. If they wanted a particular item outside their budget, they simply took a photo and wrote down the amount and put it in the box. If they still wanted it after 2 weeks, they bought it. You can imagine how much excitement an expense would have to generate to overcome being stuck in a box covered with photos of the dream for 2 weeks! He says this step was key to helping them reign in their "emergency" spending and unexpected expenses.

When willpower and automation fail

You may feel some resentment toward your taskmaster self as you begin to live on a tight budget, especially before your savings start really accumulating in the Vault. This is normal. It is also really weird because you know you're doing something good for yourself and you might hate yourself a little bit anyway.

You know, like exercise.

Consistent exercise will give you a healthier body whether you like doing it or not, and so will saving money. And like exercise, over time you will start to see the financial results in your Vault, make the connection from your daily actions, and begin to appreciate the workout that gets you there.

Until then, though, you're in a danger zone. Let's talk about how you can work through it to get your buns of steel (whoops, wrong book!)

Don't let your hard work run off the rails due to a lack of planning in the simple, everyday things in life.

But if it does...

What happens when you overspend, fall off the wagon, splurge on something you later regret, or just plain get tired of cooking and order a pizza? Lightning won't strike, the world won't come to an end, and the birds will still be singing when you wake up the next day. Only you will know this happened, and only you will be impacted (along with your partner, if you have one).

This is a precarious time because it can trigger a bigger backslide if you don't nip it in the bud. When you make a plan for screwing up, when you expect it to happen, it will be much easier to recover than if you assume you'll be perfect. In this instance, planning for failure is a very good thing.

Successful dieters know that the key to staying on track is getting back on your diet plan immediately after you make a mistake. You don't wait until the next day or the next weigh-in. You do it immediately without punishing yourself or going through any long kind of blame game. The same thing works for staying on a budget. You overspend one day, and you immediately go back to your regular saving habits. You don't wait until the next Monthly Financial Review, the next payday, or even the next day. You get right back on the program immediately without too much blame or hoopla.

You screwed up. Now you're back on track. Boom! See how fast that can happen? The trick is to recover quickly, because the longer you linger over your misdeeds the easier it will be to wallow in your indulgence and look for more or let your guilt send you on a downward spiral.

How to Recover Quickly from a Screw-up

You know it will happen, so prepare a recovery plan now.

- **Make a Deal** Make a deal with yourself when you overspend that you get five minutes to get yourself back on track. That means the pizza delivery gets eaten, but you go into the kitchen to make sure you have the ingredients for tomorrow night's dinner so it won't happen again. In fact, you may want to go ahead and prepare it so you'll just have to reheat it tomorrow.

- **Take it back** If you make a purchase that is outside your budget, take it back. Believe us, you will not enjoy wearing/using it when you know it's keeping you from your overall goal. You will always know that you blew the budget to get that item.

- **Take action and avoid blame** Focus on one action that will get you back on track, like reviewing your Dream Porn or checking your Vault balance. If you bought concert tickets and they can't be returned, sell them on Craigslist or Gumtree. Don't get caught up in the guilt or punishment of what you did. The secret to getting back on track is action. Just like research and long planning sessions are killers to getting started on a savings plan, so is navel-gazing and taking hours to work out why you did something wrong.

We are human, so of course we had screw ups along the way. The secret to our success was getting right back on track with the plan even after these things happened and avoiding the blame game with each other for occasional slip-ups. The reverse is also true:

Don't blame anyone else for your mistake. Own it and move on.

How did we recover from our screw-ups? Read on to find out.

About nine months into our savings plan, I was at a business conference in Dallas. Because the conference was focused on women entrepreneurs, there were plenty of smart marketers set up to sell non-business things to these successful women: clothes, jewelry, lingerie, credit cards, vacations, etc. I took a tour around the floor my first day there and came through unscathed. After all, I was a pro at this saving thing!

The next day's lunch was served at the center of all the booths in that giant room, and afterward I walked around again with two colleagues who were not on a tight budget. They tried on jewelry, jackets, scarves, and all the other things you would expect. And like all women who shop together, they pulled out things they thought would look good on me, urging me to try them on.

At this point it would be easy for me to blame them for my next action, but it is not their fault. I am the one in control of my spending, and I set myself up to be in a place I should have avoided, with people who had more disposable income than me. The warning bells should have been going off in my head, but the gentle clinking of the chandelier earrings swaying on my earlobes deafened me.

Me, a woman just a year away from traveling the world with a backpack and only five outfits, decided to buy a fancy pair of dangly earrings. I'm not sure when I thought I'd be wearing those – with my cargo pants and flip-flops on a beach somewhere, or with my hiking boots as I climbed a mountain? To top it off, I bought a scarf to go along with them – because every woman needs a beautiful silk scarf to wear over her cotton T-shirts, right?

The conference ended the next day, and I guiltily took my treasures home. I ended up giving up the scarf in my Reverse Birthday Party a few months later (read about this in Chapter 16), and the earrings now live at my mom's house. I wore them a total of three times before we left on the trip.

How did I recover from this overspend? Well, I couldn't take them back, so I immediately went back on the plan and tried to find other ways to save during the month before we came up for our Monthly Financial Review (we'll cover how to do this in Chapter 14). I had to cut back in other areas of our budget to make up for the over spend, which meant a heavy hit to entertainment and other non-essential expenses. The work it took to make up for that overspend – and the guilt for depleting our much-needed entertainment fund – far outweighed the feeling I got from wearing the earrings, and it really wasn't fair to Warren to have to make up for my over spend. It was a very good lesson.

Create a Phrase to Save

Use the following questions to develop your own Phrase to Save.

What are the smaller components to your dream?

- Monetary units
- Progress units like pages in a book or hours in a degree (that can be calculated monetarily)
- Distance for journeys or athletic endeavors (that can be calculated monetarily)

Can you visualize reaching any of these milestones?

- What does it look like?
- Does it make you smile?
- Can you imagine these units stacking up in your Vault?

Is it something someone else can easily see?

- Could someone else visualize it without a lengthy explanation?
- Would you feel comfortable repeating it in front of others?
- Would you feel comfortable having your savings partner recite this to you when you're weak?

Use your answers from the above questions to generate your own Phrase to Save. Below are some ideas to help you.

- **Blatantly copy our idea** and set up a 'days to X' for your goal

- **Visualize the physical components of your dream** For a house or a business, focus on the building blocks. "This week we bought 2 doors!" or "My new business can now afford to buy me an office chair." You don't actually buy those things right now, of course, but visualizing that you can will help you continue saving until you do.

- **Set up your dream in stages** If you want to write a book and your dream is to save enough money to stop working while you do, map out how long it will take you to write a chapter or a page and the equivalent living money you need to do so. You'll be really jazzed as your novel takes shape over time ("I've saved enough to write 57 pages; the plot thickens!")

If you have trouble coming up with your Phrase to Save, recruit your friends and family to help. The important thing is to find a visual image and smaller number that you can easily reference in your daily life. Without it, you're climbing up a very big hill with no handholds along the way. You're going to get tired.

So, what is your Phrase to Save?

Make sure you create an effective one, because you will be using it a lot in the coming months.

Chapter Summary

The Phrase to Save is a powerful tool in the Action Plan for Dreamers. It is a quick reminder of the long-term goal you're working for when a more immediate desire is in front of you. The Phrase to Save is a unit of measure of your dream, a way to whittle down that big savings number into something you can visualize in your daily life. Otherwise you'll be tempted to justify $20 here and $20 there throughout the month because it is such a small percentage of your overall goal. When it is a percentage of a much smaller number, you'll be more likely to stick with your budget.

The Phrase to Save isn't bulletproof, of course. Sometimes you will screw up because you are human. When you do, the key is to get back on track immediately, not the next day, week, or month. Just like exercise, the longer you wait to get back on your plan, the harder it will be. Creating a "failure plan" when you feel strong will help you recover quickly when you are weak.

Take the time now to create a Phrase to Save that resonates with you, one specifically tailored to your dream. The better you make it now, the more effective it will be when you need it. It is easy to confuse what you want most with what is available in the moment, and the Phrase to Save will help you keep it straight.

Now that you have a Phrase to Save, you'll get a chance to apply it to your current spending in the next chapter.

Chapter 11: Analyze and Cut Expenses

"I find it fascinating that most people plan their vacation with better care than they do their lives. Perhaps that is because escape is easier than change."

~Jim Rohn

Once you start looking at your current financial situation, it is easy to see why you weren't able to save any money. Perhaps you ate out a lot like we did, or you got in the habit of buying new clothes each month. Maybe you haven't looked at your insurance coverage in a few years and realize you're over-insured, or you're subscribed to several things you don't even use anymore. You may even be surprised to find out how much it costs to own and maintain your vehicle(s). And do you really need a $200/month cell phone plan?

It can be pretty overwhelming to see it all in black and white, but this painful piece is the start of something wonderful.

You can give yourself a night to sit with the information from your initial dump of financial data, discuss it with your partner or a friend and let your mind start calculating ways to reverse the trends as you sleep. At the very least, you should be working on your revised

Roadmap tomorrow morning. Don't sit on this too long. Like research, it can kill your progress by keeping you in a holding pattern. The key is action.

Pour yourself a cup of tea – or something a bit stronger if you need it – and come back here when you're ready to start creating a new Roadmap to get to your Dream. (Don't worry; we'll wait.)

Now is the time to start analyzing expenses to revise your Roadmap, but before we do that we'll let you in on some of our dumb spending habits and tough choices so you know you're in good company.

Speaking of dumb spending habits...

C'mon, tell us the most embarrassing place you spent money last month. You're among friends. (You can even hashtag it #DSDconfession on Twitter or Google +.)

The most embarrassing for me during our first budget calculation was the $8/day I was spending at the drive-thru on the way to work. Over the course of the year, I spent $2000 on a crappy breakfast ("bear claw and a Boston cream plus coffee with cream and sugar, please") to start my day and got an extra bonus along with it: a weight gain of 10 pounds. That was not a wise spending move, though it did seem convenient. Looking back, I could have easily put a carton of yogurt with some granola and a piece of fruit in a bag at home and eaten at the office, saving the cash outlay, the 10-minute diversion from my commute, and the expanding ass. Hindsight is 20/20.

(Maybe we should call it "behind" sight.)

We can laugh at these things now that we've saved the money and my ass is smaller than it ever has been, but you may be feeling a real worry about giving up some of your expenses, even the ones you know are not good for you. This is human nature, and we don't like having someone tell us what to do (even if that someone is our "higher" self trying to break through). In his book, *Do the Work*, Steven J. Pressfield introduces us to the concept of our higher selves (the ones who want to do great things) and our lower selves (who want to do what is easiest). The book is centered on the idea of resistance, the force that arises when we are at a critical point in our path to change. Resistance is your clue you are on the right track, even as it compels you to abandon your plans. You'll face resistance as you make changes to your habits and your spending to get to your dream, and knowing ahead of time what this means – that you are on the right track – will help you 'resist the resistance.'

How You Soothe Yourself Through Spending

Akiyo used to think money was there to spend. She said, "you get X amount every month and you keep spending until it is gone." If she had some left over when a new payday arrived, she felt she hadn't quite lived to the fullest extent with her money. She managed to save a tiny portion, but her main goal was to use her money up and exchange it for as much stuff as she could get. (Before you criticize this attitude, look around and realize how much it permeates your own life.)

It wasn't until she started working toward her dream that she realized money could give her life, "not breathing, heart-beating life, but a life that sees things, hears things, tastes things – really living." Once she realized her spending was keeping her from the life of experience she wanted, possessions and indiscriminate spending no longer gave her a thrill. She told us, "I now spend money to live and I see myself as something worth investing money into."

You may not be able to see it now because you're at the starting line, but you will look back later and wonder how some of these things ever meant anything at all to you in comparison to living your dream. If you're living a life not true to your dream – in more ways than financially – sticking with the status quo will only get you more of the status quo. You won't find your dream if all your money and attention is going to soothe the dissatisfaction with your current life. You have to start looking toward what fits instead of constantly adjusting what doesn't. Let us give you a sneak peak into our former lives to show you what we mean.

Back in 2004 we bought a house in the Boston suburbs – a giant house for us, actually. Three bedrooms, four bathrooms, a fully finished walkout basement, two-car garage, large yard backing up to the woods with a multi-level deck for entertaining. We actually paid a lawn maintenance service to take care of the yard in the summer and plow the snow on the long driveway in the cold Boston winters. (Without it, we would have had to buy and use a snow blower to get to work most winter days.)

For two people who didn't want children, spent all their time working and traveling, and just wanted to relax in their time off, this sounds like a really dumb move, doesn't it? We thought we couldn't afford to live in the city, so instead we bought a huge house in the 'burbs that cost the same as a city apartment and took on all the maintenance and commuting costs associated with it.

Dumb, dumb, dumb. We were trying to let our income dictate our lifestyle instead of the other way around.

We spent weekends shopping at the home outlet stores, buying a bunch of crap to fill up the house that was too big for us. We had to drive for at least 30 minutes to be anywhere, and an hour to be anywhere with lots to do and people like us to do it with. We purposefully placed ourselves an hour's drive away from all the things we found fun and invigorating – culture, diversity, friends, restaurants open after 8 pm – and then set about firmly cementing ourselves into that uncomfortable space.

We tried to fit in with the young families that surrounded us, but you can imagine how much we had in common with them. At my first neighborhood book club meeting I made reference to the fact that I had gotten divorced when talking about a point in the book we were discussing. Silence descended over the room. I could have been anything else in liberal Massachusetts, but in a small enclave of families with children, divorce was still a big no-no. I was not invited back for another meeting.

I joined another group to play a dice game called Bunco, which seems to be a fairly common "girls night out" kind of thing in neighborhoods across the US. Because I didn't grow up in the area or have kids that went to school with the other moms' kids, conversation lagged pretty quickly. I was invited back for this game again, but it was mostly because I was an easy mark and lost every hand, because I certainly didn't add to the conversation. I was a fish out of water, and it was obvious to every single person but me.

We were each trying to make ourselves comfortable in an uncomfortable space by spending money, playing the part of the lifestyle we chose without ever considering that it might not be working. Our strategy was to buy and accumulate to fit in instead of looking for the place we would naturally fit in.

It wasn't all doom and gloom, of course. We loved our couch, our bed, the way the sunlight streamed into our bedroom in the morning through the curtains. The big chair by the window in the office was perfect for reading, and the painting we bought on vacation looked dramatic on the chocolate-brown wall in the dining room. Yes, we loved all those things.

We also loved the smell of the grass after it had been cut and enjoying a hamburger from the grill on the deck on a sunny afternoon. The house was beautiful, and we enjoyed getting compliments from the neighbors on the new exterior paint job.

Eating out whenever we wanted was a luxury neither of us had growing up, and we liked not worrying too much about the prices at the mid-range restaurants we frequented. Being on a first-name basis with Rick the wine shop owner, who recommended a nice bottle for us every weekend, was also a nice perk. It made us feel important and almost like we fit in. We *liked* spending money freely and responding to all the urges that came up in our reptilian brains, even if we didn't enjoy our job commutes or live close to our friends. It was a nice consolation, or so we thought.

But you know what? Even if you took all those things that we loved about the home and combined them into one giant fantastic feeling, they still would not compare – or even be in the same category – as the feeling we have every single day now as we live our dream.

The activities and experiences you have now either work for you in getting to your dream or they work against you. Even items and activities you like now may not fit into your dream, and that's okay. We may not get to sit on a sunny deck and enjoy a hamburger at our house anymore, but we do get to enjoy a variety of sunny decks and exotic meals in countries all over the world. It's a definite trade up. We enjoy Argentine or French wine in the countries where they are produced, so we don't need to become best friends with the wine shop owner. As house sitters we have stayed in homes far nicer than the one we owned, or more modern, or right in the city center, or even once a houseboat! We don't have to own the perfect home because we have the opportunity to try all the versions of the perfect home as we travel the world.

When you start thinking about your expenses, your activities, and your purchases in relation to revising your Roadmap, keep your finish line in mind. Do these same expenses, activities and purchases fit in the Dream you have waiting for you? If not, it might be time to consider reducing or doing away with them.

> *Change is hard. Change is also what takes you from where you are now to where you want to be.*

We're going to show you how to cover the distance with as little pain as possible, though once you reach the finish line you'll barely even remember it. Trust us on that one. Now let's talk about the so-called "necessities" that are keeping you away from your dream.

The Choices We Made

> *"Don't tell me what your priorities are. Show me where you spend your money and I'll tell you what they are."*
>
> ~James W. Frick

You know what we hated about being on a tight budget for 25 months?

- Coloring and cutting our hair at home
- Wearing the same damn clothes for two years straight
- Giving up our favorite shows on cable
- Eating at home instead of our favorite ethnic restaurants

- Not taking a real vacation for 2 years

At first we had a lot of resentment about giving these things up.

DIY Haircare

"Because I'm worth it."

~ L'Oreal

Have you ever colored your own hair? It's messy and it stinks. The first time I did it, Warren pointed out that I had missed a giant section in the back. Two–tone hair. That's what you get for not using a professional.

Over time it got better, but it certainly was never the experience you get at the salon – peaceful music, a nice scalp massage at the shampoo bowl, and a gorgeous blowout and style at the end. You leave the salon looking and feeling like a million bucks. When you color your hair at home, you finish with wet hair and a pressing need to clean the bathtub before it stains.

Warren took it a step further and began cutting his own hair. Standing naked in the bathtub, he buzzed as much as he could and then asked me to finish the back. The first time this happened we ended up fighting because I didn't press hard enough with the razor, so he grabbed it from my hand and accidentally shaved a bald spot in the back of his head.

After I stopped laughing at him and wiped the tears from my eyes, I realized all the hair had gone down the drain. Time to get the drain cleaner. Over time we worked out a better system for this that didn't cause fights or plumbing problems.

Total savings over 25 months: $2850
Days on the Trip: 28.5

Nothing to Wear

> *"Distrust any enterprise that requires new clothes."*
>
> ~ Thoreau

You know that jacket you love so much right now? Or the pants that fit you just right? Two years later, after wearing them every single week, you won't love them nearly as much. In fact, you might even hate the sight of them. When you choose not to buy accessories to jazz them up, or new shoes to update the look, even your favorite current clothes will lose their shine over time.

Your friends will show up in cute new outfits, tell you about the great deals they got shopping over the weekend, or dazzle you with their funky jewelry from a local designer – things that make your mouth water and your knees weak, and all you can do is compliment them.

Warren worked in a really casual environment, which meant wearing T-shirts most of the time. Have you seen what happens to a T-shirt that gets worn regularly for 25 months? It's not a pretty sight. The underarms get stained, the neck begins to unravel, and the body loses its shape.

Lucky for us, love is blind. After 25 months, we could hardly remember the attractive, put-together people we used to be.

Total savings over 25 months: $2500
Days on the Trip: 25

Turn Off the Boob Tube

> *"TV is chewing gum for the eyes."*

~ Frank Lloyd Wright

Before we started saving for our dream, you could count on the fact the television was on every evening we were home. We saw no problem with this in general. Watching TV at night was relaxing. We could shut off our brains after a long day of work and just absorb without any contribution required on our part. We loved television.

The day I called to cancel our cable the exchange went something like this:

> "I'd like to cancel our cable, please."
> "Where are you moving? We can arrange for it to be turned on at your new place now."
> "I'm not moving. I'm just getting rid of cable altogether." (Silence)
> "What are you going to do for fun?"

What made it worse was discovering that as long as we still had the cable box, it wasn't going to be turned off. Those sneaky devils at the cable company had their hooks in us and weren't going to let go easily. We had to disconnect it ourselves and take it back to them to finally stop service, and even then they let us know we could have it turned back on anytime. They told us they were leaving a note on our account to waive the reactivation fee.

We felt like we had just been on an episode of Intervention as we left the cable office. (See, even our references were TV-related.)

Savings over 25 months: $1800
Days on the Trip: 18

Dining In

> *"My wife dresses to kill. She cooks the same way."*
>
> ~ Henny Youngman

When we moved to Seattle from the suburbs of Boston, one of our requirements was to live within walking distance of at least nine ethnic restaurants. We loved moving to the funky little neighborhood of Fremont with Cuban, Thai, Indian, Chinese, French, Japanese, Belgian, Mexican, and Vietnamese restaurants not far from our front door. We were never at a loss for delicious food – until we started cooking for ourselves, that is.

I'm not sure I can express to you how much I love food: the flavor, the texture, the way ingredients combine together to form something new in your mouth. It is almost sexual, this love affair I have with food. The light grows softer, the air becomes more fragrant, and sexy music plays in my head as I savor the flavors and textures of a delicious meal. I have even been known to make little noises of pleasure while eating. (Yeah, weird isn't it?)

When you're not a good cook and have to prepare your own meals, this love affair with food becomes less like a romantic evening and more like masturbation. It gets the job done, but it is certainly no substitute for the real thing.

> *Savings over 25 months: $18,750*
> *Days on the Trip: 187.5*

Stay at Home

> *"When you look like your passport photo, it's time to come home."*

~ Erma Bombeck

The big dream in our life was to travel. We were giving up a lot to realize this dream, most importantly any actual travel for the duration of our savings period. Sure, we could take the occasional outing or weekend trip, but the days of flying off to Europe or even across the country for fun were over. Hot summer in Seattle? Too bad, we weren't going anywhere. Finally fed up with the gray winter by February? Sorry, no sun for us.

Our friends went on fabulous trips – Hawaii, Mexico, skiing, wine-tasting, cruising – and we stayed at home.

Savings over 25 months: $5000
Days on the Trip: 50

How We Discovered Our Dream Fund

During all that time, we continued asking ourselves the **Phrase to Save:**

> *"Is X (clothes / salons / TV / restaurants / vacations) more important than X day(s) of living our dream life?"*

In every case it wasn't, but that didn't take away the sting of not getting what we wanted. Not having the money to do something is one thing – we've all been there. But having it and not using it, well, that's a new muscle getting used.

Maybe this evidence will convince you:

Total Savings from these 5 conveniences over 25 months: $30,900
Total Days saved for our Trip: 309

We won't kid you: this plan is not for the weak-willed or faint-hearted. You will have to say "no" to many of the things you use for comfort now, which is doubly hard when you consider how uncomfortable you'll feel at first.

If you're ready to accumulate some serious cash in your life to fund your dream, you have to be prepared to make choices, pay attention to your money in big and small ways every single day, and fend off the peer pressure to spend and blend into the crowd.

To create an extraordinary life, you have to make some extraordinary changes.

If you aren't ready to do that, put this book down now. It won't do you any good. If you're ready, though, you'll come to some of the same kind of conclusions we did:

- **Hair** My hair looks pretty good with a few strands of gray, and it makes travel a lot easier when I don't have to worry about finding a salon every 6 weeks.
- **Fewer clothes** mean easier packing and less weight in the backpacks. You can't be a clotheshorse and travel long-term.
- **Television** is now a thing of the past. We can enjoy a show or a DVD now and again, but we've seen so much in our travels that entertainment via box is a very poor substitute.
- **Ethnic restaurants** We now call those local restaurants. We eat delicious food every day

in countries around the world, discovering new delicacies every week.

- **Vacation** Sure, we lived without one for two years, but now we live one 24/7/365.

The things you think you want so much in your life now – entertainment, convenience, decoration – might be the same things that are holding you back from living the life of your dreams.

Keep this in mind as we tackle the first revision of your basic Roadmap in the next chapter.

Ideas to Cut Your Expenses

We've already talked about how we made some changes to our spending, but here are some more ideas for your own budget modifications. Check out our website at www.DreamSaveDo.com/#resources/ for more resources on saving money.

Rates and Fees

- **Call your cable** company and let them know you're going to have to cancel and find a cheaper option if you can't get some kind of better deal. They will often offer you a 3- or 6-month reduction on your cable bill if they think you're going to leave. Your best bet is to cut it altogether and free yourself of the monthly expense as well as the cost of giving your evenings over to nonproductive activity. But if you aren't ready for that yet, this is a good start.

- **Analyze your last three cell phone bills** and see if you're getting close to the maximum allowed on your plan for minutes / roaming / texts. If you aren't, or if you know you can reduce it, then call them up and lower your plan. Since these plans change frequently, it is wise to check in every once in awhile to see if there is a plan better suited to your needs, saving you tons of money in the meantime. Second tip? Don't upgrade your phone at the end of your contract. The one you have now will suffice until you get to your dream deadline and you can go month-to-month on your existing plan usually without being locked in (if you don't buy a new phone, that is).

- Are you paying bank fees? Simply keeping your money should be bonus enough for them, so if you're paying fees find out why. **Call your bank** and get these fees canceled or find a bank that will not charge them. The same goes for your credit cards. Why pay a fee when you're paying the balance off every month (and you're now paying them off every month, right?) For excellent tips (and scripts) for negotiating with your bank check out the site:

  www.IWillTeachYouToBeRich.com

Subscriptions

- A quick scan of your credit cards, PayPal account and bank account will alert you to monthly subscriptions. Are you still using those services? It's easy to let a few $10 or $20 fees accumulate every month, and before long you're paying over $1000 year for things you don't even think about or use (gym membership, anyone?) **Make sure you're using what you pay for or get rid of it.**

- Magazines and catalogs and sales fliers are going to derail your savings plans. **Cancel them now** and save yourself the temptation. You can opt out online at:

  www.catalogchoice.org

Insurance

- We often don't look at our insurance plans to check for coverage. In fact, we often over-insure "just to be on the safe side." It pays – literally – for you to spend some time reviewing your home, auto, life and health coverage to find out if you can **reduce your premiums**. We saved hundreds of dollars per year with one phone call after finding out we qualified for a "recreational driving" insurance plan for putting less than 5,000 miles per year on our car. We also found out we had some duplicate coverage on our townhouse because the HOA insured part of it, so we were able to reduce that coverage as well.

Track cash spending

- **Carry a small notebook** with you to track any cash spending. If you think this is a waste of time or a drag, then you're obviously spending too much. It should only be a few entries a day at most, and it will help you see where some of that money is going. Watching the money disappear and then tracking it in a notebook has a way of making you pay attention to what you're buying.

Food

- One thing we tried while saving was **bulk cooking**. We could make several dishes on a Sunday – double sized – and then break them down into smaller portions to freeze. We only had to take a couple of containers out every few days to defrost, make up a salad or veggie dish, and we had a healthy, delicious dinner in no time. This idea came from our personal chef friend, who did it for clients all the time. Just don't forget to label your food with reheating instructions or you'll have "surprise supper" every night.
- Bulk cooking makes you think about bulk shopping, right? Well, we are against this idea because it leads to spending money on things you won't use for months (or years, in some cases). **Buy what you need for the week/month.** No more. Your extra money is better spent accumulating interest on your dream than on the latest sale items you don't immediately need.

Clothes

- The only clothes permissible on such a tight budget should be for children, and that is just to replace what they've outgrown. For you, for your partner – what you have now is what you keep for the duration of your savings plan. New clothes will not help you save or keep your mind focused on acquiring your dream. Avoid malls, magazines, and catalogs and you will be surprised at how quickly the urge to buy new things settles down.

- Because some of you are really sneaky devils looking for a loophole, we're adding shoes, accessories, and jewelry to the clothing restriction. Just in case you didn't know. (wink-wink)

Books

- If you're big readers like us, then you probably have a lot of books and can't imagine giving them up. But what if giving them up meant access to even more? By **selling your books to a used bookstore**, you free up your space for more books and give yourself a large credit to use in buying more books in the future. Think of it as your current investment in books financing your future reading. Most bookstores in the US offer a larger in-store credit than they do a cash payout for books, so if you're a big reader this is a great way to finance your reading during your savings plan. (If you haven't visited a used bookstore lately, you're in for a treat. There are lots of great titles old and new available for a fraction of the original price.)

- How long has it been since you've visited your **local library**? Times have changed, my friend. No longer do you have the little index card with inky stamps and signatures for checkouts. Today's libraries have online resources and eBooks, you can often reserve your books online and then just pick them up, and there are a variety of DVDs, CDs, and other resources available at the click of a button. In addition, inter-library loan is another resource. If you haven't visited your local library since you got out of school, now is the time to find out what you've been missing (and what your tax dollars have made available for you).

Movies

- If your idea of good entertainment is a movie, then you're in luck. **Netflix** and companies like that offer great deals for movie lovers. You can even stream some movies on your computer with a subscription to one of these services. The price is set no matter how many movies you watch per month, so this could be a great money-saver if you're a movie buff. The bonus is that you no longer have to wait long for new movies to make it to DVD - usually only three months or so.
- If you've just gotta see a movie at the theater, check into the **matinee rates**. We were surprised to find a significant savings by attending the weekend morning movie at 10:30. After breakfast, you probably won't want a big bucket of buttery popcorn or chocolate, so your temptations at the snack bar will be minimal. Good for your budget and your bum.

Transportation

- If you live in a moderate-sized city, you will have access to **public transportation** options. Check out your options for car sharing, commute sharing, buses, subway, train and tram service where you live. When you factor in the costs of your current driving, you may be surprised to see how much you can save by using a combination of the above options and good old-fashioned foot-to-the-pavement or bicycling. We saved a lot of money by changing our transportation choices, so this is well worth a look for you. Don't just shrug it off because you like the independence of driving. We did, too, but after changing to this method we don't know that we'll ever own another car again. There is a certain kind of inner peace that comes from never having to look for parking again. Check it out.

Travel

- Travel? How did this get on the list!? Well, even though you can't travel extensively while on a tight budget, there are times when you find a great budget way to do it and times when an emergency comes up and you have to do it. We were able to go in with friends to rent a cabin and share cooking/grocery duties during a long weekend a few times during our savings plan. Camping would have been even cheaper if we hadn't already sold our gear. **Consider group travel with friends** as a way to lighten the financial load and have more fun.

- **Frequent flier miles** are a great asset to have, and during an extreme savings plan these can be lifesavers if an emergency comes up. I had one such flight to visit my family in New Mexico and the miles we had saved paid for it completely. A last-minute ticket bought with cash would have been extremely expensive. If you have frequent-flier miles, save them during your extreme savings plan for moments such as these. If you don't use them, then you have something else to look forward to at the end.

Phones

- We talked about this briefly above under Rates, but there is more you can do about this expense. **Does everyone in your home have a cell phone?** Then why do you need a landline? Check out your options for 911 services via cell phone, and if this works for you then drop the landline. Bonus? You'll stop getting telemarketer and political calls instantly. (You're welcome.)

- Need to call long distance and waiting for your evening and weekend rates to kick in? Bypass all of that and **switch to Skype.com**. You can make all your calls online for free (with or without video), and if you need to call to a regular phone number the rates are fairly cheap. Basic membership in Skype is free, so anyone you talk to regularly can have it set up and ready to go in just two minutes. If you're still making long-distance phone calls with a landline or eating up your minutes on your cell phone plan, check out this option.

- This is the painful one, the one you might object to most. But hear us out, okay? **Do you really need the cell phone and/or plan you have now?** We've already established that you won't be upgrading during the extreme savings process, but you're always free to downgrade. Think about what you truly need and decide whether the extra dollars you're spending for the bells and whistles are truly worth it for you. We've been without a cell phone since October 1, 2010.

Medical Care

- Are you taking advantage of all the medical checks available to you? In the US most insurance covers preventative medical care, such as dental cleanings and cancer screenings like Pap smears. Do not neglect your basic medical care, especially when it's covered by your insurance. Letting these things get out of hand is what will cause a major health crisis – and possible financial meltdown if you live in the US – and prevent you from living your dream after working so hard to save for it. Extreme saving does not mean skimping on your health care.

Exercise

- We've all joined a gym at some time or other in hopes of becoming fit and lean. Most of us lost our commitment to going to the gym before the ink was even dry on the membership card, but we continued paying for it anyway in hopes that some day we'd regain our enthusiasm. Just forget it. If you haven't used it by now, you won't. Explore options for exercise that are more fun that sweating it out alone on a grimy machine. Walking is great exercise and can be done anywhere at any time. Take it up a notch and start hiking in your area, challenging your legs to get you up a hill and back down. You can pack a lunch and make a day of it, invite friends and family members, or join a group of walking enthusiasts and make new friends. Best of all, walking and hiking are free. If you have a bicycle you can get your exercise in much the same way. If you want to become a runner you can start with the excellent Couch to 5K (www.c25k.com) program. Aim for fun when you work out – swimming, tennis, dancing, etc. – and you'll stick with a program a lot longer.

Cheap vs Frugal

- Keep in mind that we are not always advocating the cheapest way to do something. It is always wise to be frugal with your money, but it doesn't always mean you'll buy the cheapest thing. If you make smoothies every day for breakfast, you need a sturdy blender that will grind up your fruits and vegetables. If you only make margaritas during your summer BBQ party, then you can get by with a cheaper version. See what we mean? Spend your money wisely.

Spending Money on Other People

Now that you know how to create a Roadmap, set up a savings account that functions like a Vault, and question all expenses, it should be a piece of cake to save the money, right? Ah, I wish it were so.

Big and small things will happen every single day to challenge your budget and lifestyle decisions. Even your friends and family will sometimes challenge your plans – knowingly or unknowingly. The key to success is planning, and one of the biggest Roadmap busters is holiday and gift spending. We justify it because it's for someone else, and that leads us down a slippery slope. Plan for your holidays and birthdays long before they happen and you'll stay happily on budget.

Birthdays and Holidays on a Budget

Guilt, habit, and social pressure make it harder to change our spending habits when it involves other people. After all, your budgeting largely affects only your immediate family and you, the same people who will benefit from the lifestyle change this money will eventually bring. But this other person who is celebrating a birthday or expecting a holiday gift is neither part of the sacrifice nor part of the windfall at the end.

What we learned during our savings plan is that the people who love and support you will understand. In fact, when your friends and family see you making big strides in your savings plan it will inspire them to do the same. There is not a week that goes by that a friend, reader, or family member doesn't comment on how our activities are inspiring them to make changes in their lives.

People really do want you to succeed (and if they don't, you need some new friends). So take some time now to decide how you will handle birthdays and holidays. Below is how we handle ours.

Plan your holiday spending now

Birthdays: We called our friends and family on their birthdays and even occasionally sang to them. For close friends who were nearby (our family all lived far away), we got together for a birthday lunch or small party with several friends. The gift was in the celebration – the gathering of friends, sharing of food and drink, and spending time together. The cost was minimal, but the memories were far stronger than any item you could buy.

If you want to give gifts to your children, partner, parents, or others, you can. Remember, this is your Roadmap. Just make sure you add in those expenses.

New Year's Eve: This is a biggie, isn't it? For those who like to celebrate this holiday, it often means a new outfit, tickets to a great party, and plenty of booze and food until midnight (and possibly a big breakfast out afterward). If you want to go out, you can do it on a budget. Wear something you already own, or shop at a consignment shop or Goodwill to find a great outfit. Better yet, trade closets with a friend so you both find something fun. Save a little bit out of your entertainment budget in October and November to add to December, and you can enjoy a night out without any guilt.

One year we took overnight bags and our dog to visit some good friends. We made a potluck dinner, combined resources for beverages, and after we watched the glittery ball drop in Times Square we had a Wii video game tournament. The next morning our hosts made a delicious breakfast of eggs Benedict, and we were home by noon. For us, it was a perfect low-cost, high-value option to the typical New Year's Eve outing.

Valentine's Day: I've written about this before. Setting aside one day a year for an overpriced romantic meal and a trinket is just plain crazy. I want love and romance all year long! So we decided early on not to celebrate February 14, but to infuse more attention and affection into our relationship every day. I don't care what you got for Valentine's Day last year – it cannot beat what we've done for our relationship throughout the year by working together on a shared goal. I hope you'll consider rethinking Valentine's Day this year in favor of 365 days of love and appreciation.

Fair warning, though. Working toward a huge goal together can be a pretty powerful aphrodisiac. I'm just sayin'.

Mother's and Father's Days: Most of us have been making gifts for one or both of these holidays since we were small children. Remember the homemade cards, pottery ashtrays, and flower pots you made as a budding little artist? I'll bet your mom and dad still have them. If you live near your parents, consider cooking them a fabulous meal at your home instead of going out. You'll be able to have a better conversation, and you can take time to look at old pictures or talk about some of your favorite times together without worrying that you're overstaying your welcome at a restaurant.

If you live far away from your parents like we did, consider going old school and make your parents cards again. A personal note from you, even via email, that reminds your parent of a special memory, your appreciation of something they have done for you, or your wishes about future plans together would be just as valuable as those old flower pots and ashtrays used to be. Trust me. Wouldn't you love to get a card or letter like that?

Independence Day (US): I love this holiday. Not only is a BBQ the cheapest kind of party, the casual nature of it means you don't really have to sweat too many details. Whether you're going to a party or having one yourself, potluck is the way to go. Almost every party we attended during our savings days included a small contribution of food, drink, or cash from the guests, and it made it easy on everyone to get together and have fun. If you can watch a professional fireworks display instead of buying them yourself, you get the view without the hassle and the cost. What a great way to celebrate!

Labor Day/Bank Holidays: Most of the expense of this holiday is travel, and if you plan it in advance you can easily fit it into your budget. Otherwise, Labor Day or a bank holiday is just as easy as Independence Day in terms of planning, except that you don't have to worry about fireworks. You can also think about small home projects or creative endeavors. One year I participated in the 3-day Novel Contest and wrote a book! Three days is a great boundary for trying something new. After all, it's just 3 days. You can do anything for just 3 days.

Halloween: We lived in a neighborhood with very few children and have none of our own, so we're not experts at saving money on Halloween. We do it by default. But we do have smart readers, one of whom told us she set up a Facebook group for parents in her neighborhood to recycle kids' costumes for Halloween and school plays. It's a big hit in her neighborhood, and it gives a great costume a longer life.

Check out your city calendar for free Halloween events. In our neighborhood we had a large troll statue (he's quite famous!) and there is an annual "Troll-o-ween" parade that draws a few hundred people each year. Festivities like this are usually free and a fun way to celebrate the holiday.

Thanksgiving (US/Canada): I remember as a child wondering how my mom could enjoy a holiday that was so much damn work for her. After toiling for a couple of days on a delicious meal, it was then enjoyed with gusto by our family and then we all turned into couch potatoes to take a nap or watch a football game while she cleaned up.

What a horrible way to spend a holiday! Of course, my brothers and I shouldn't have been such brats to enjoy her hard work without help, but that's another story.

Thanksgiving is another great potluck opportunity, whether you're hosting or attending. It allows each person to show off his or her "specialty," no one works too hard, and everyone helps with the cleanup. When everyone takes part in making the holiday successful it seems like attitudes are better and people try harder to make the celebration special.

A tradition that I love is to go around the table and have each person state one thing for which they are grateful. It brings the thanks back into Thanksgiving and doesn't cost a dime.

Black Friday/Christmas/Boxing Day: Some people love the excitement of shopping for big deals the day after Thanksgiving, and other people dread it but do it anyway to save a few bucks.

Guess what? You can save more money by having a smart strategy. I used to spend hours shopping for the perfect gift for everyone on my list. I was usually tired, cranky, and over budget by the time I finished each shopping trip.

The holidays are meant to celebrate your connections with family and friends, not to send yourself into debt. Would you want someone to worry about paying their bills in January because of a gift they bought you in December? Then why would you do that to yourself?

Set up boundaries with your family and friends several months in advance of the holidays so everyone is on the same page. When I moved away from my family we decided that my visits home and their visits to me would be far more valuable than any trinkets we could buy for each other. Warren and I don't exchange gifts with anyone but our parents, but you may come up with an idea that includes a dollar limit, drawing names, or buying one gift for the entire family.

While we were following our Action Plan for Dreamers we spent our time seeing our friends at holiday gatherings, calling and sending cards/emails to those far away, and enjoying our tradition of Chinese food on Christmas day followed by a movie. We did not venture into a retail store between Thanksgiving and New Year's Day, and our sanity and bank account remained in balance. It was a lovely way to enjoy the holiday season, and we had no fear that January's bills would send us over the edge.

Our way of celebrating may not work for you, and that's okay. The point is to demonstrate that you can enjoy celebrations without breaking the bank if you do a little planning. When you make out your budget, think about how you want to spend the holidays and what it will cost to do it, and then factor that in.

Having a plan is half the battle, and knowing you have control of your finances will allow you to relax and enjoy your time with family and friends. Isn't that what it's all about?

Chapter Summary

To change your life, you have to make changes. The habits you are holding on to now – out of comfort, security, or ease – may be the very actions keeping you from your dream life. By reviewing your expenses, you can see how your money is moving you closer or further away from the life you want to live and make adjustments.

You'll be surprised to find out how much of your dream money is hiding out in your current spending. Once you identify the areas you want to change, review our list of money-saving ideas to see how you can make it work for you. Remember, you don't have to make all your changes at once, and sometimes a step-down approach is more effective (we'll talk more about that in the next chapter).

When it comes to the other people in your life, you may find it more challenging to save money. The important thing is to have the conversation about your budget early so others know why you are changing your gifting habits. For more ideas on how to save money and cut expenses, visit our resource page at:

www.DreamSaveDo.com/#resources/

In the next chapter, we'll start morphing your current budget into the Roadmap that will take you all the way to your dream.

Chapter 12: Develop Your Roadmap

"Nothing can stop the man with the right mental attitude from achieving his goal; nothing on earth can help the man with the wrong mental attitude."

~Thomas Jefferson

Now that you know what your spending looks like by category – even though you may not want to look at it – you can get down to the nitty-gritty of where to spend and where to save in your first "revised" Roadmap. This is where you will start estimating your spending and saving to get you to your dream. And if you have a partner, the decisions can get complicated.

- Your wife wants to keep her $150 hair appointments every month, even though you're in over your head in credit card debt.
- Your husband plays golf every week to the tune of $100, not to mention all the golfing accessories he likes to buy.
- You both love to eat out, have hectic jobs and can't imagine cooking at home every night.

You may also be surprised to find out **where** you're spending money, and creating a budget can sometimes start arguments over where the money has been spent in the past, bringing up hidden resentments and old fights.

> *"I can't believe you have been spending that much money on your fingernails!"*
> *"Well, I'm the one who does all the cleaning around here, so I deserve a little pampering!"*

You get the idea.

The important thing in the budgeting process is to look forward. Your past has passed, and there is nothing you can do about it.

Consider the goal you both have in mind and go from there. When you're both focused on a specific amount and each party makes equal sacrifices to get to that goal, you go back to being a team again. And isn't that why you chose your mate in the first place?

And if you're single, try not to be too hard on yourself. What's done is done, and luckily you only have yourself to bust into shape. Though your alter ego can be a pretty tough adversary when she wants to be.

How to agree on a budget roadmap

- **Have a mutual goal** – See Chapter 3 for more info on this.
- **Give yourself some "mad money."** Everyone needs a little cash they don't have to account for to anyone else. Your mad money may be $10/week or $100/week. Doesn't matter, just make sure you have some and don't get mad when your mate spends his on things you consider wasteful.

- **Agree on a regular review** to make modifications to your budget. Do this every month.
- **Build in some variety.** You won't feel deprived about less eating out if you're sharing a romantic picnic on your living room floor or enjoying a sandwich and a good book in the sunshine at a park on a sunny afternoon. Be creative.
- **Think about do-it-yourself options.** You can color your own hair, wash your own car, and mow your own lawn.

Shared sacrifice means shared victory.

For us, the goal is a mutual one, but it wasn't always that way (see the charred remains of our first marriages for lessons on how to work separately on opposing goals). You have to be able to compromise with your mate on both the goal and the way to get there so neither one feels bullied into doing something.

If you're single, you get to skip the compromise and do it all for yourself. This means you can live really lean in one area that's not as important to you while still maintaining one that is. It's a good trade-off, and you can take advantage of being the boss of yourself to make these unconventional spending decisions. (When Warren was single he ate cereal for dinner because it just wasn't important to him to cook after work every night.)

When you reach your goal, you will be so glad to have worked through your difficulties with your partner or your alter ego and celebrate your success. Money issues really can bring you closer together if you work it out as a team, and reaching a goal like this is a huge motivator for you as an individual as well as a couple.

Believe us, if you can save together, you can do anything together.

Evaluate your personal spending habits

You already have your Dream and your Phrase to Save, and this is where you get to use them both to combat your wasteful spending as you create your first budget Roadmap in Mint, MoneyDashboard, SmartyPig, Quicken, or whatever system you have chosen. They all have easy budgeting tools and tutorials to answer any questions you may have. The hard work is in gathering the information and facing your current spending, which you've already done. (Remember, if it is easy to use you'll actually stick with it. Don't overcomplicate the process by making this harder than it has to be.)

Now is the time to ask yourself what you want more, the item/service you have listed in your Roadmap or your Dream. You can clarify any tough decisions by using your Phrase to Save. A few words of wisdom: Just because you need something like food and shelter does not mean you necessarily need them at the level you have them now. Don't give these "necessities" a pass on the question. You can live in a different place, drive a smaller car, take public transportation or walk, bring your lunch to work, downgrade your cell phone plan, get rid of your land line, live without cable, and "make do" with your existing electronics instead of always getting the upgrade.

Ask yourself the question for every single expense category on your budget Roadmap. If it makes the cut and stays, does it stay as is or could it do with some adjustment? If it goes, what is the plan for cutting it and the deadline for doing so?

How to Change Your Spending Habits

If you're feeling overwhelmed at this point at the thought of changing your spending so completely, then you're normal. We understand because we were there, too. We have three strategies to share with you to make it an easier transition (and remember what we said about easy – always aim for the easiest solution because it is the one you're most likely to continue.)

Make your changes in stages

Start with one category of spending that needs to change and do it for one month. You'll be more comfortable with it by then so you can move on to the second category. Keep going in this fashion until your budget is finalized. The key to this is to map out the stages at the beginning so there is no dilly-dallying at the start of each month. You have a lower risk of backsliding because you only concentrate on one thing at a time. This is a plan for reasonable people, and you will reach your goal in a reasonable time. If you're an unreasonable person, you'll want to speed it up and tackle a few categories at once. Time's a wastin'.

We initially focused on our transportation budget, parking our car in the garage and using public transportation or walking 85% of the time. We changed our insurance coverage to "recreational use" because of the low mileage and saved hundreds of dollars per year. We also saved hundreds on gas and maintenance costs. It was a way to gradually get us used to a car-less lifestyle, so by the time we actually sold the car we were ready for it. It would have been too drastic of a change to sell it on day one of our Action Plan.

Do an initial sweep to take 10% off your total spending across the board

Every three months, do another sweep to take out another 5 or 10% from your expenses. This strategy is similar to the above but more generalized across all your spending. How can you reduce spending from every category by 10%? This is how corporations reduce budgets. Another option is to apply higher percentage cuts to the least vital expenses (do you really need a landline if everyone else in your house has a cell phone?).

We were able to take continuing cuts in our grocery spending as we learned to cook better, in our entertainment budget as we became more creative, and in our insurance as we began discovering how much duplicate coverage we had.

Put your budget together and then start it in 3 months or 6 months or after the big vacation or when school is out or, or, or...

There is never a perfect time to do anything in life, including a budget. You have to make it the right time. Your dream requires action, and if you aren't ready to commit to action it won't do you any good to finish reading this book. (Come back when you're ready; we'll be here for you.)

Be ruthless. This is what it takes to save large amounts of money in a short period of time. It is not a forever way to live, but it is a way to get to "happily ever after" sooner than you ever imagined. If you're serious about saving a lot of money in a short period of time, you can make big progress fast. If you want to be more moderate, you will have less discomfort but for a much longer period of time. It is your choice as to how fast you want to start your dream.

The goal is not to have a perfect Roadmap at the start, but to have a workable one that is continually refined every month until you have the perfect balance of saving and living.

You will learn to love your Roadmap because it is the tool that is bringing you closer to your dream. Fall in love with it, caress it, say nice things to it, and show it plenty of attention. Find creative ways to save. Make your budget happy to see your face at your monthly review date and it will show you plenty of love in return.

Speaking of Saving and Spending...

This is also a good time to analyze your relationship with advertising and realize it is an S&M relationship whether you like it or not (and yes, you're the masochist in this scenario). Let me explain.

The mail was wrapped inside a bulky catalog as I pulled it from the box. It was surprising to see a Crate and Barrel catalog after so long with no magazines or catalogs.

"It won't hurt to thumb through this." Or so I thought.

We were already starting to purge our possessions in preparation for our trip around the world, and we had already made the decision to sell the house before we left.

This is why my reaction to a fancy lemonade dispenser was so unexpected. I knew we were leaving all our possessions behind. I knew we were going on a trip around the world. And frankly, I don't even drink much lemonade.

But I wanted it. I kept the catalog on the bar and even showed it to Warren. He looked at me like I was crazy, and in the moment I probably was.

"Do you think that will fit in your backpack?" he said. *Smartass.*

Even though he was right, and even though everything about my life and decisions said I shouldn't want that damn lemonade dispenser, I did.

I put the catalog in the recycling bin and took it out right away. But even now, years later, I still remember the visceral want for something I knew I would never even use.

Would I have even thought about a lemonade dispenser that day if I hadn't received the catalog? Of course not. And I definitely wouldn't have considered buying one. That is the power of advertising, and the only way to successfully fight it is to remove it from your life.

Advertising is more powerful than you think. Don't rely on your willpower. If you don't tempt yourself, there is no chance of failure.

How to deflect the power of advertising

- **Remind yourself of the Phrase to Save:** "Do I want this more than I want my dream?" You're going to wear this little jewel out. Having this question on the tip of your tongue will get you out of most dangerous situations.

- **Avoid temptation** You know what triggers your mindless spending, so don't even go there: malls, furniture stores, restaurants, bookstores, gadget makers, shopping websites. The same goes with magazines and catalogs. Get rid of them, and you'll be surprised at how much easier it is to avoid temptation. Outta sight, outta mind. Window shopping is not allowed.

- **Plan your day in advance** Know what and where you plan to eat, how you plan to have fun, and when you'll be back home. If you leave it up to chance, you will overspend. These add up over time and take away from the money you could be saving for your dream.

Do you get the idea that you need to plan for these temptations before they come up? Your willpower alone is not enough. Don't make yourself work any harder than you have to.

Planning is the key to saving an extreme amount of money in a short period of time. Yes, it is hard work. Yes, it requires constant attention. If it were easy, you would have already done it by now, along with everyone else. But it's not; it takes planning and commitment to make it happen. You know you can do this.

Chapter Summary

Creating your Roadmap is a powerful process. With the click of a few buttons, you can see how changes in your daily life impact the finish line to your dream. If you are working with a partner, this Roadmap helps you align your goals and set expectations for actions and spending throughout the month. If you are single, it is a way to boldly experiment with what you really need and want as you save for your dream.

There are 3 strategies for making changes to your current spending:

- Focus on 1-2 categories at a time for spending cuts
- Make 5-10% spending cuts across the board
- Wait til the perfect time to start (hint: there isn't one.)

Remember, it's your Roadmap.

Last, it's important to appreciate the power of advertising. By taking yourself out of harm's way – avoiding the shopping malls and eliminating catalogs from your life – you'll have far greater success against indiscriminate spending.

We've now finished part II of the book. You've learned how to set up your savings account, calculate your current spending, address your credit card debt, create a Phrase to Save, cut your expenses, and refine the Roadmap that will take you to your dream destination. In the next section, DO, we'll show you how to take some actions to support your dream, including making some extra cash, monitoring your progress monthly, and recruiting the support of your family and friends.

Section III: DO

where you take your evangelism to the streets, combine your saving with action, and teach your friends and family how to support your big dream

Chapter 13: Produce Additional Income

"The biggest mistake people make in life is not trying to make a living at doing what they most enjoy."

-- Malcolm Forbes

One cash-amassing monster of an idea is earning a side income. Before you throw up your hands and say you don't have the time – or desire – to take on more work, hear us out. Your second job can be something you actually like to do, something maybe even related to your big dream. You don't have to scan the classified ads for this type of job. Your only boss will be you.

You remember Samantha the fancy cake decorator. Her dream and her side job were one and the same. She had been practicing her hobby for so long she had a demand for her services before she had way to supply it. This is every entrepreneur's dream, and it made the small up-front investment easier to manage since she had a revenue stream from day one.

Chris Guillebeau wrote about this in *The $100 Startup: Reinvent the Way You Make a Living, Do What You Love, and Create a New Future*. When you match your interests with a need, you can often make better money than you could at a traditional part-time job, along with setting your own hours. In fact, it is usually something you would do for free anyway.

Chris's book is chock full of case studies of people just like you who took their skills and passions and turned them into a business, often getting them off the ground for $100 or less. One example is Gary, an amateur "travel hacker" who earns hundreds of thousands of frequent flyer miles every year through airline promotions. He's a whiz at both accumulating these miles and using them to create fantastic vacations. But since he has a limited amount of vacation time and a regular job, he was only using his skills to plan a few trips a year. He began branching out by helping friends, many of whom were business travelers racking up lots of miles but with no clue how to use them. (Airlines don't make it easy.)

Gary began charging $250 to plan dream vacations for people with more frequent flyer miles than know-how. This might seem crazy - after all, he's being paid to set up something a person can do themselves for free - but if you've ever tried to book even a basic flight with miles you know how complicated and limiting it can be. Imagine trying to do this with a multi-destination vacation or dream trip. Gary makes it easy for people to use the miles they have accumulated while indulging his love of travel planning. This side hobby now brings in six figures in income. Yes, you heard that right: he makes more than $100,000 per year from his side job.

Another example is former music teacher Brandon, who created an interface, a small "front end" to his website, to help him schedule students and perform billing. It saved him in administrative work - work he wasn't getting paid for - and allowed him to concentrate on teaching. Over time, he realized the problem he solved for himself would be attractive to other music teachers and he began selling it as Music Teacher's Helper. Teachers quickly saw how it would save them money over the long run, and Brandon now finances his life in Costa Rica from the sale of Music Teacher's Helper.

These are two great examples from Chris's book of creating a part-time job for yourself. In the first case, Gary shared his expertise with other people for a price, essentially renting out his brain to people who didn't want to invest the hours in learning the intricacies of airline rewards programs. Brandon solved a problem for himself and saw how other people could benefit from his same solution.

Look to Your Skills and Interests for Ideas

Are you a whiz at Twitter and Facebook? Partner with a social media company to manage these accounts for some of their clients, or go directly to the industry of your dreams – traveling, extreme sports, snake charming, whatever – and see how you can parlay those talents into helping people who are already doing what you want to do. There are plenty of people out there who want this kind of help and will pay for it, and you get the bonus of earning money in a field that is related to your dream anyway.

Much better than flipping burgers.

Say you want to be a full-time writer. Are you good at editing, writing magazine stories, ghost writing blog posts or books, or even writing advertising or sales copy? There is a part-time job out there for you if you look. You can write on your days off, or for an hour each evening.

You'll remember Matt from earlier in the book. To help fund their Indonesian sabbatical, he and his wife started two part-time jobs: a product photography business for him and a wholesale bakery business for her. He was able to book clients on weekends, and she was able to land a consignment deal with the largest Asian grocery store in town for her pastries. They each pursued a hobby they loved for very minimal cash investment and setup.

Warren started building websites as a hobby. I needed a site for my consulting business, and he built it. When some of my entrepreneur friends asked me about my site, I referred them to him and he built theirs, too. At first he did it as a favor while learning, and then people started buying him gift cards in payment, and finally he realized this was a viable business. He began charging to develop basic Wordpress sites with the goal of teaching the business owners how to update and maintain their own sites. It was a great arrangement because these solo entrepreneurs had more ideas than money, and by giving them a way to showcase their new products, special sales, and discounts, he was giving them more control over their business than they ever had before. The projects were typically shorter than a month and he was able to do 2-3 per month.

Warren's initial clients referred other people, and before we knew it, he was fully booked and had earned enough extra money to pay for two tickets on a cruise to Antarctica – something that would have been outside our travel budget otherwise. Would you build a couple of Wordpress websites a month for a year to go to Antarctica? Of course you would.

None of the above ideas may appeal to you, or they may be outside your skill set. No problem. These examples are designed to generate ideas about how you use the skills and interests you have right now to work within your dream industry/field/area of interest and make a little cash to go along with it. You may be surprised where it leads you.

For us, learning how enjoyable it was to make extra money this way was a game-changer. Website development wasn't part of Warren's career or something he ever considered doing for money, but it was something that made a fairly big impact on our savings plan and something he continues to do to this day. Your part-time job might just give you a little extra "pocket money" even after you've started living your dream.

Design your own part-time job

Can you think of a skill you have that can be used to generate some cash? Below are some ideas and success stories to help you brainstorm:

- **What is the thing that you're known for?** Creative mom Nicole Donnelly turned a practical need for airing out the bottoms of babies with diaper rash into a multi-million dollar business called BabyLegs – all because other moms noticed the little arm- and legwarmers she created for her baby and asked her to make extras[3]

- **What is it you always have an opinion on?** Dany Levy loved scouring for information on her city – all the best places to shop, eat, relax, and rejuvenate. She took a gamble that not everyone had the time or inclination to do all that work, but many people were interested in the results. The result is the original "daily offer" company, Daily Candy[4].

- **What questions do people ask you?** If you're the "go to" expert on a subject for your friends and family, consider how you can turn that skill into cash. Robert Stephens began the 20,000-employee strong Geek Squad as a college kid making house calls on his bike to fix computer problems and hook up stereos[5].

I'll bet none of them expected the level of success they attained, and they all started by selling something they were already good at or doing anyway. You can do the same as you amass the cash for your big dream.

Here are a few more ideas to get you started courtesy of the freelance gurus at Passive Panda:

- **Dog walker** In some places you can get $25/hour for this, and when you realize that you're also getting your daily exercise at the same time, you can forego that membership to the gym you aren't really using anyway. Read how two women in different locations do it: www.PassivePanda.com/dog-walker/.

- **Translator** If you know more than one language, you have a leg up on most of the population. Use your skills to translate documents, websites, and books. Read how one man makes $150/hour doing this www.PassivePanda.com/freelance-translator/.

- **Proofreader/editor** Are you the kind of person who loves books like *Eats, Shoots, and Leaves*? You can make a nice side income as an editor. Read how one woman has been freelance editing for 20 years: www.PassivePanda.com/proofread/

What is your special talent and how will you use it to finance your dream?

How to Handle Found Money

You can also add to your savings with unexpected money. I'm not talking the lottery (please tell me you're not throwing your hard-earned money away on that). I'm talking about birthday money, bonuses from work, tax returns, and even the slim possibility that your cousin Jimmy finally repays the money you loaned him 10 years ago.

There is also another kind of "found money" and that is hidden in the junk sitting around in your garage, spare bedroom, and closets. If you have even the slightest motivation to dust that stuff off and sell it on Craigslist or eBay, you can add a nice chunk of change to your savings account. (We made over $8,000 from selling our junk on Craigslist.)

I'm betting that old junk doesn't have a place in your new dream life anyway.

However the found money finds its way to you, you have to be prepared. It is tempting to spend the $20 you just made selling your old Xbox games on a pizza delivery – it's only $20, right? And most people figure out where they'll spend a tax return before they even have the money in hand. What about birthday money? Your grandma is probably going to ask you on the spot what you'll do with that $5 she just tucked into your birthday card.

The hardest money to keep from spending, at least in our experience, is the bonus money from a job. You worked so hard for that – above and beyond your normal duties – and it can seem like you're bypassing your reward by not getting a little something nice for yourself.

These moments of excess, whether you expect them or not, are both a blessing and a curse. You have the opportunity to put a chunk of change toward your goal, yet you have been living lean for a while now and just want to reward yourself a little bit.

Go stand in front of your Dream Porn for 10 minutes and visualize living your dream life. This is the time to remember why you're saving money in the first place.

This isn't a rainy day savings account. This is a specific account to finance a big dream, and every time you delay putting money into it, it puts your dream just a little bit further away.

Your lifestyle will only be like this for a very short time in the grand scheme of things. But if you continue to spend your found money, you will stay right where you are.

Remember your Phrase to Save: "Do I want this more than I want my dream?"

How do you handle Found Money? Most importantly, don't handle it at all. Move it directly into The Vault.

In most instances, you shouldn't be surprised when you get money. Using online calculators, you should be able to estimate your taxes pretty well no matter what country you live in, and if you're getting large tax returns or credits each year it would be smart to figure out why.

In fact, you can go one move better and get your tax return money throughout the year instead of giving the government an interest-free loan. (You know that's what you're doing, right?) According to MSN Money tax expert Jeff Schnepper, 52 million Americans received an average income tax refund amount of $3,082 in 2010. That's $160 billion lent to your government for free while you're using your credit cards to scrape by every month. It hardly seems logical, does it? Adjust your tax withholding so you are paying the appropriate tax and getting your 'tax refund' every single payday. Your Vault will get fuller and you'll get a bit of money in interest, to boot.

Bonuses from work probably come around at the same time every year, and while you may not be able to pinpoint how much it will be, you can psyche yourself up to put it toward your dream instead of a new flat-screen television.

Gifts, and the off chance that cousin Jimmy will repay his old loan, are harder to handle because they often come during a celebration or time with family and friends. You're already in a festive mood, and it may be harder to think about putting the money in the Vault.

This is where the Phrase to Save will come in handy:

"Do I want this pizza/dinner out/television more than I want my dream?"

Probably not.

Our Experience with Found Money

We experienced "found money" frequently during our savings plan, mainly because we were actively selling our possessions every week as part of our process of downsizing to prepare for our own Dream.

Every week we had "found money" – sometimes as little as $5, a few times as much as $500. There is something that happens when you're holding cold, hard cash in your hands. It was a little bit harder for us to think about transferring that money every time, and because we were dealing mainly with strangers buying our possessions via Craigslist, we always asked for cash instead of checks. (Find out more about how we made $8000 by selling our junk on Craigslist.)

We made a plan to handle the found money by instantly – and I mean immediately after closing the door to the buyer who just picked up their item – transferring it to The Vault. We went online and transferred the cash amount from our checking account into The Vault. We could then leave the cash in the house to be deposited into our checking account later or use it on our everyday expenses as needed. There was no temptation to "blow it" because we had already put it in The Vault.

You have to make it easy on yourself. The less you touch the money, the less likely you are to divert it from where it needs to go.

The best way to handle found money is to have a plan. Immediately transfer it or set a specific date for it to go directly into **The Vault**.

Chapter Summary

You can fast track your savings (and maybe even the path to your dream) by creating a side hustle. It doesn't have to be elaborate or expensive, and the smart move is to focus on what people want from you right now.

- What do you know how to do that your friends and family don't?
- What do you like to do that nobody else does?
- What do people come to you for on a regular basis?

By realizing your talents and interests have a ready market, you can determine the right kind of side business to make extra cash.

The other additional income you can count on during your Action Plan for Dreamers is found money. This can come from birthday gifts, tax refunds, selling your junk, or bonuses from work. You may not always know when you're going to get it, but you should have a ready-made plan for putting it into your Vault when you do. In addition, examine your tax withholding status to make sure you aren't floating loans to the government every year. Better to have the money throughout the year so you can earn a little interest on it.

In the next chapter, we'll start bringing all the pieces you've learned together to perform a monthly financial review. This is your monthly check-in with your dream, and it will keep you on track until you reach the finish line.

Chapter 14: Perform Monthly Review

"My problem lies in reconciling my gross habits with my net income."

~Errol Flynn

Warren sat at the kitchen table with the laptop evaluating our budget out loud while I bustled around the kitchen cooking dinner.

> *"We went over on groceries this month."*
> *"What? How can that be?" My mind started racing, thinking of how that could have happened.*
> *"I'm just telling you what it shows."*

I could feel the blame in his voice since I was the one who did all of the grocery shopping. It was going to be a tense dinner tonight. I racked my brain trying to think of where that money could have gone. We hadn't done anything out of the norm, had we? I stirred the pot and mentally reviewed the month's grocery trips. Then I remembered: Book Club.

This monthly gathering with my friends was always fun, and I looked forward to the potluck dinner, wine, and good conversation all month. The previous month, however, I didn't plan very well and ended up on book club afternoon with nothing prepared for the evening. You know what happens in that kind of scenario, right? You overcompensate for your lack of preparation by over-buying.

I cruised the aisles of the gourmet grocery store near my friend's house on the way to book club that night. Why couldn't she live near a regular grocery store, the kind where people actually use coupons? Like every unprepared person since time began, I was laying the blame on other people for my mistake. (Why does Una live in a cave so far away from the good hunting grounds? Grunt.)

The sample servers were out in force with their samples of delicious food, and hungry office workers were streaming into the store to stock up for the weekend. I was both empty-handed for book club and running late. Meanwhile, I was mentally calculating how much time it would take me to finish shopping and make it through the long checkout line.

I dashed around the store buying wine and an assortment of dips, creams, and varieties of hummus along with crackers and chips. To ease my nerves I bought a Diet Coke as well. I did actually stop myself from buying flowers for my friend, though just barely.

My lack of preparation for a long-planned evening cost $43 – $33 more than I usually spent on a homemade dish for book club night, $33 that could have gone into our savings plan, $33 that was equal to 1/3 of a day on the road. I had just given up an entire afternoon in a foreign country by not being prepared for a book club that was on the calendar for a month. It didn't take me long to figure out the rest of the over-spend for the month, and it was all due to lack of preparation or rushed buying.

Identify Mistakes and Move On

You may think that's a little overdramatic and nit-picky, but if you want to save a lot of money in a short period of time you have to think that way about your spending. If I continued with the same attitude and behavior the other 11 months of the year on book club night, I would have cost us at least 4 days on the road.

To Warren's credit, he did not play the blame game with me. If you're saving with a partner, you can't afford to focus on each other's faults, either. The only way to be successful is to present a united front, so it's really important to be dispassionate about the occasional mistakes on the budget, learn from them, and move on.

Regular mistakes on the budget – or one person ignoring it altogether – are another matter. You both have to be invested in the goal and the plan to save money for the dream in order for this to work. It doesn't mean there won't be times you mess up or feel weak, but it does mean you quickly get back on track after each flub because you want that end goal so much. If one of you is not working toward the goal, you'll never reach it together.

I learned my lesson about how quickly a lack of preparation can throw the budget off track. That was a small hiccup of a mistake that kept us from making bigger mistakes down the road.

Nip bad behavior in the bud.

What is a Monthly Financial Review?

In order for your Action Plan to generate the results you desire, you must monitor your progress. The best way to do this is a monthly financial review of your Roadmap.

This is when you sit down without distractions to review your spending and saving for the previous month. Your online financial dashboard will make it very easy to see the numbers. You then evaluate what went well, what didn't go so well, and what changes – if any – to make for the next month (upcoming events, expenses, holidays).

If you are saving with a partner, it is very important to remember the lessons on principled negotiation from Chapter 3. This is not a time to blame or martyr. It's a time to dispassionately review your budget like a business (because it is the business of your dream). You focus on what went well and how to continue it as well as what went wrong and how to improve it. Take your emotions out of it, because they will not serve you well here. Put on your business cap and leave it on til you're done.

There are some ground rules to make it easy and painless. Let's review them before we get started.

- Pick a low-stress time for your review – on a day off, after a good meal, etc.
- Acknowledge mistakes, learn from them, and move on. No flogging allowed.
- If you're saving with a partner, review with your partner.
- Perform your review in sight of your Dream Porn.
- Create a post-review ritual to celebrate your success

Perform a monthly financial review

How do you set up a monthly financial review? Simple, you just carve out a half-hour window to review your spreadsheet or your online dashboard with Mint or MoneyDashboard. Next is a handy set of questions to use in evaluating your results.

Enter figures into budget spreadsheet for the month, either in your own personal budgeting software / spreadsheet or an online solution like Mint or MoneyDashboard.

- Don't forget to enter your cash spending from your notebook.
- Be sure to break down credit/debit card expenses into specific categories to better track spending.
- Don't forget to review your savings – this is the best part!

Did your spending fall within projections?

If not, why?

Did you go over in a category?

If so...

- Does this mean you need to adjust your budget, or is it a one-time thing?
- How can you prevent this next month?
- Did you adjust your spending in another area to make up for it?

Did you underspend in a category?

If so...

- Remember your occasional expenses like insurance and gifts. Just because that block is empty doesn't mean you were under. (You would be wise to break those yearly expenses down into monthly estimates to keep your budget on track.)
- Should you adjust your budget item down permanently, or was this a one-time thing?

- If the trend is going down, can you eliminate this item altogether?

Is there anything on your budget that surprises you or seems out of proportion – either higher or lower – to the rest of your spending?

Analyze these findings to further refine your budget.

How does your spending compare to last month, or the last quarter?

You can spot trends this way and decide whether a budget item can be permanently decreased or eliminated altogether.

Did your savings fall within projections?

If so, congratulations! If not, why? And how will you get back on track – specifically – for next month?

Plan your expenses, activities, and obligations for the next month.

Planning is your best defense against temptation

- Do you have gifts to buy, repairs to make, or any other non-recurring expense coming up?
- Are you expecting any "found" money to come your way (bonuses, gifts, etc.)?
- If you're saving with a partner, lay all your cards on the table. Do not make it a surprise at next month's review.

Make any necessary adjustments in your budget.

Remember that your budget is a living, breathing thing and should be updated as needed.

- Adjust for any decisions to decrease, increase, or eliminate a budget item.
- Adjust expectations in savings for "found" money.
- Adjust your checking account automatic transfers to The Vault to account for any new money you have freed up for savings.

Give yourself (or each other) a high-five for completing a month of savings for your Dream!

Create a post-review ritual that celebrates your accomplishment.

- An energizing activity like a walk or a bike ride
- A relaxing and indulgent activity like a long bath
- A special meal or treat that is only prepared on monthly financial review day

Notes on the monthly financial review

Remember that your budget is a living, breathing thing. It requires constant upkeep to stay alive and can be expanded or shrunk to fit your needs.

In fact, this is a great little "lesson within a lesson." Once you master a really tight budget for a short period of time, you can continue to use it the rest of your life with only minor tweaks to reflect your current level of spending.

It's easy at this point to get mired down in the details of your expenses, but it's even more important to focus on what you have saved. Even an automated savings that you can project with confidence should be confirmed each month.

Better yet, convert your Vault balance to the thing that you want the most by using your Phrase to Save. In our case, it was "# of days on the road." Every month we could see how many days were in our balance and imagine what we'd spend our time doing with them when we hit our goal. Do not underestimate the power of this exercise.

Chapter Summary

Monthly review of your Action Plan is vital to staying on track for your dream. By logically evaluating what went well and what didn't, you can continually refine your Roadmap every single month and anticipate events that will impact your spending or saving. Forewarned is forearmed.

Remember the ground rules for a successful monthly financial review:

- Pick a low-stress time for your review – on a day off, after a good meal, etc.
- Acknowledge mistakes, learn from them, and move on. No flogging allowed.
- If you're saving with a partner, review with your partner.
- Perform your review in sight of your Dream Porn.
- Create a post-review ritual to celebrate your success

Use your online financial dashboard (Mint, MoneyDashboard or your own spreadsheet) to make the process easy (remember, the easier you make it, the more likely you'll keep doing it). If you're working with a partner, make sure you are in alignment about your financial goals for the upcoming month at the end of your review.

In the next chapter, we're going to learn about peer pressure, social support, and asking for help. While money might be a big component of your dream, it's not the only one. You can't do it alone, and thankfully you don't have to.

Chapter 15: Establish Social Support

"Really great people make you feel that you, too, can become great."

~Mark Twain

It feels like there should be some confetti and celebration at this point. You've taken your fuzzy notion of a dream and clarified it so much you can put a price on it. If you have a partner you've included him or her in the planning. You gave your dream a worthy name and created some Dream Porn to fuel your desire. A Vault was built to house your dream money, and you've ironed out the specifics of your spending and saving on your Roadmap. That along with the Phrase to Save and your Monthly Financial Reviews is going to lead you on the direct line to your dreams.

Yes, you should have confetti and a party right now. But what does that require? Yep, you've got it: Other People.

Telling People About Your Dream

When you share your goals with other people, you get the benefit of using their brain space and connections. Your friends, coworkers, acquaintances and family members will contribute ideas you never considered, open doors previously closed to you, and give you moral support when you need it. Telling other people is part of the reason why you created such a great name for your dream back in Chapter 4.

But it won't be all sunshine and roses, and we're going to talk about the positive and negative reactions to your news and how to handle them both. The key thing to keep in mind is that people's reactions are generally about them and not about you. Once you get that clear, it's a lot easier to let the comments roll off your back and keep moving forward. (It also makes you feel like a voyeuristic psychologist in a way, so don't dwell on your friends' hang-ups too much!)

Think about it; someone who is obsessed with personal security is going to be fearful of your goal of moving to the big city. A lazy friend might try to derail your daily workouts as you train for an Ironman event. Your shopaholic sister may have real anxiety over your new minimalism.

On the flip side, your adventurous friends will revel in your big challenges. Other parents will applaud your decision to start a family. Healthy family members will support your goal to get fit.

Are you starting to get the picture? Your biggest asset and your biggest potential downfall in creating your dream lies with the people you know and love. Your family and friends usually have your best interests at heart, but you have to remember that those interests are colored with their own perceptions of what is good for them (and you).

Perception is reality. Proceed accordingly.

You won't get the support of everyone, but you will get a lot of support and should count on and expect it. People love to see a big turnaround, a success story, or an overcoming-the-odds scenario. If they can help you make it happen, even if it is something they wouldn't do themselves, they will usually do it.

Remember, you don't need anyone's permission to chase your dream. You've already made up your mind and you're simply sharing the good news, period.

How to Spread the Word

The first people to tell are your closest supporters, people you know will be there for you (even if it takes them a few minutes to digest the news). You can do it in the way that best suits your current relationship (in person, over the phone/Skype, over email), but make sure you give them time to ask questions and become comfortable with the news. This is very important because once they have your back, it won't matter what anyone else says.

Once your top-tier support is in place, it's time to tell other people. Depending on your goal, you may be keeping the news quiet from your employer or other Dear John recipient in your current life, and that's okay. But your behavior and spending will call attention to you sooner or later, so you're better off beating them to the punch. Sharing your news is always better than defending your decisions.

Consider an energetic Facebook announcement when you know you'll have some support of your top-tier friends. Others will see their support and get the message this has been vetted already. People love to jump on a bandwagon, and when there is social proof it makes it easier.

You can also email your friends to let them know, share your Dream Porn on Pinterest, or even set up a blog to keep them informed as you progress toward your goal. That's what we did; the popular personal growth website Married with Luggage started out simply as a way to keep our moms informed of our progress. Whether you decide to publicize your dream to that level or not, you will find it helpful to keep some kind of journal or blog of your experience. You'll be amazed at your progress over time, which will motivate you to keep going.

Managing reactions

Your good friends may be excited to see you embark on your dream and cheer you on, but these same friends may resent the financial restrictions on your social life. In part this is because it impacts them as well, since you won't be able to join them for some activities due to cost.

The other reason is that it highlights the differences between you and them. Without meaning to, you're making a judgment about their lives because you've chosen to do something different than what you did before. You may be saying, "I'm so excited to do this," but the other person is hearing "My life is better than yours because you aren't doing this." It's not usually even a conscious thought, but it does bubble just under the surface.

If you don't believe us, think about the last time someone's comment annoyed you. Was it really what they said, or what you thought about what they said? There's a big difference.

You may find some friends are resentful of the implied judgment that they should make changes, too, and they go about casually – or forcefully – undermining your plan. This is a tricky situation because neither side sets out to do this. In fact, a lot of it is unconscious. But it does happen – frequently – and you have to be prepared for it.

When Akiyo told her fellow PhD graduates she was turning down the lecturer's job after graduation, they were confused. How could she walk away from this great job after working so hard to get her degree? In truth they weren't really thinking about all the late nights Akiyo spent writing her thesis; they were thinking of all the work *they* had done on theirs and reeling from the decision that someone could walk away from it. It went against everything they trained for, and they didn't understand it.

Sometimes the reaction is based in fear of missing you, either because you're changing something substantial about yourself or you'll be busier or in a different location. Parents and family members are most often in this category, and it's hard to shake the guilt of forcing them to make a change to their lives because you want to do something different. Parents especially are good at laying on the guilt! But no one can 'make' you feel guilty. Those feelings come from your own expectations of right and wrong, and to change them you have to change your mindset about your worthiness to live the life you want.

Brenda had a similar issue with her father. She decided after being downsized from her media job to finally create her dream of living and working overseas. Her 40th birthday was approaching, and even though money would be tight, she knew she could swing it. She'd been dreaming of this for years, saving money for the day she might make it happen, and this black cloud of job loss seemed to have a silver lining to it.

She told us the biggest problem was her father, who didn't want her to move away from her neighborhood in

New York City, much less leave the country. Brenda was very close to him and didn't want to disappoint him, which is why she had kept her dream on the back burner for 20 years already. The only roadblock in her plan was her father, and it made the otherwise-independent Brenda embarrassed this was such a problem. (We were also surprised this straight-talking woman couldn't stand up to her loving but controlling dad, though we shouldn't have been. We all have these relationships to a degree in our lives.)

Once she decided to do it, Brenda began removing her roadblock piece by piece. She told her father she'd be spending some time in South America while she waited for the economy to improve but didn't give him a timeline. As the weeks went by, she'd continue dropping information about what she planned to do, and when her father began asking more detailed questions she'd give more information as if it was the continuation of a conversation they'd already been having for weeks – because it was. Brenda made it harder for him to dispute the decision when he finally learned she was moving permanently because he'd already been hearing about it for weeks without protest.

She knew it would be difficult for her father to adjust to this news, so she gave it to him in stages, letting him get used to it a little bit at a time. It didn't solve her problem completely, but it did make it an easier transition for them both. Brenda is now living in Brazil, teaching English, and in love with her Brazilian boyfriend. Her father recently came to South America for a month-long visit. He's still not crazy about the idea, but he accepts it because he can see it is what she really wants in her life.

Your friends and family will too.

Unmet expectations

We were excited to take a weekend trip with another couple to a nearby city. It had been a tight few months of saving, and by scrounging a bit here and there we were able to gather enough money to stay in a budget hotel and see the city. Our friends knew of our budget and plans to travel, and we were surprised when they agreed to a less expensive trip than the type we had taken together in the past. We researched hotels and found one that seemed to meet both of our requirements and excitedly awaited our trip.

When we arrived, our friends were not happy with the hotel. It was a fine basic hotel, but they were right in the assessment that it wasn't as nice as their usual holidays. For a getaway, they wanted a bit more luxury. So did we, but we knew going into this weekend getaway that was not a possibility. Still, for them it was not a pleasant surprise.

They reluctantly agreed to stay so we set down our bags and took off to see the sights. We like to explore on foot, both for the exercise and the cost savings, and we were soon pretty far away from the hotel. Our friends wanted to stop for a drink and then take a cab back to the hotel to get ready for dinner. Taxi? Drinks in the chichi part of town? And then dinner? We were planning on drinking the bottle of water we filled that morning and walking back to the hotel before going to dinner.

You can see where this is going.

We gave in because we felt like we were ruining their weekend. It never even dawned on us that they could be ruining ours because we were the ones who had changed the rules. So we stopped at a trendy bar and had a drink outside on the patio in the sunshine. Which turned into another drink. Which turned into appetizers to stave off hunger. Which turned into dinner because the night was so beautiful and we had a prime table at the corner of the courtyard and could see every other restaurant in the area was mobbed.

To top it off, we took a cab back to the hotel.

When I look back at the pictures from that night I see a lot of discomfort in the faces around the table. Our friends thought we had conned them into a weekend with no fun, and we thought they were trying to derail our budget.

We did not come to a clear understanding before we left on what to do and how much we could spend, and it wrecked our weekend and put a severe dent in our friendship. We went way over budget out of guilt, a desire to fit in to our old lifestyle, and having unclear expectations from the start. To them "budget" meant something completely different than it meant to us, and it was our fault for not making that more clear.

It was our last big trip with those friends, and over time the invitations to movies, dinner parties, and happy hours with them trickled away to nothing.

I don't blame them, and I don't blame us. It simply comes down to the realization that not everyone will go along with your budget, and frankly they don't have to. This is your decision, and when it impacts the lives of those around you they can choose to go along with it or not. You have no choice in the matter, and you can't be angry with them for not wanting the same things as you.

It's not all doom and gloom and a friendless future, though. On the plus side, some friendships will blossom and new ones will be created.

Expanding Your Social Network

Several years ago, we lived pretty large. We had two good incomes, and after moving to Seattle we had very little debt. We weren't ridiculous with it, but we also didn't hesitate to accept or initiate dinner invitations, buy drinks for friends, or spontaneously plan a weekend away.

For our friends with equal means, this was great. For our friends who either had less money or chose to be more conservative with their funds, we didn't get to see each other as much. We were the friends who didn't think too much about spending money, which is why we had such empathy for these kinds of people once we started our budget.

It helps to be able to understand both sides of the situation.

Once we started our budget, we began socializing in a different way. We had more dinners at home or invited people over for a glass of wine on the deck at the end of the day instead of meeting at a bar. We took the ferry on a sunny afternoon to enjoy the view instead of dining at a restaurant with a view. We went to the morning matinee instead of the evening movie.

The nice thing about living this way is that more people are able to socialize with you. When we shrunk our entertainment budget, we increased the number of people we could spend it with.

Our social life grew dramatically during our savings period. We shared expenses to create parties together. We cooked brunch on Sunday morning instead of going out. We had slumber parties with food, drink, and games on New Year's instead of going to the bars. We went shopping together at the farmer's market on Saturday mornings instead of the mall. We took advantage of free events like community concerts, and we told each other about great deals when we found them.

These friends were excited to see us save, and they took many of our suggestions to use in their own budgets. It became almost like a game, and everyone in our circle knew of our $100/day goal for travel. They repeated our Phrase to Save almost as often as we did!

When you gather the right people around you, your restrictions on your spending can open up a world of riches you never knew existed before.

Setting Expectations

The next time we decided to go on a weekend trip with friends a year later, the experience was completely different. It was early spring, and we were feeling that overwhelming sense of gloom many people in the Pacific Northwest feel when they have been under gray skies for three straight months. We wanted to get away, but we knew our options were limited to nearby areas. And what nearby area was both inexpensive *and* sunny? We thought we were out of luck.

We were expressing our frustration to a close friend who suggested a weekend trip to Sequim, Washington, a small town on the Olympic Peninsula. Sequim gets an astounding amount of sun because it is in the "rain shadow" of the surrounding forests. Our friends mentioned wanting to go, too, so we decided to plan the trip together.

Learning from our last mistake, we were upfront with our friends as to our specific budget and expectations for a weekend away, and they agreed. Warren spent a week searching all the home rentals in the area until he found the perfect one with two bedrooms at a very low price. When we split the cost of the rental with our friends, it was an extremely affordable option for a weekend getaway. We agreed that we would divvy up the costs of food preparation and that our main activities would be hiking, relaxing, and playing games at the house. We even assigned who would be cooking what meals so we had everything set before we left Seattle.

We each brought our dogs so we didn't have to pay for a kennel. Another plus was being with another dog-loving couple that didn't mind – and actually enjoyed – traveling with pets.

We enjoyed a glorious weekend of sun, eagle watching, hikes around a beautiful body of water, and plenty of good food, conversation and fun. This is the kind of vacation we would have never considered before, and now I can hardly think of a better way to travel with friends.

We ended our weekend getaway with a little sun on our cheeks, probably an extra pound or two around our waists from all the good food, and funny photos of a good time with great friends. There is not one memory around this event that makes us regret a single cent we spent.

I could recount dozens of similar experiences, from backyard barbecues to free outdoor concerts to the popular "soup night" we started at our house (where everyone had to show up with their own bowl and spoon as a mock of our newfound minimalism). When your good friends see how much you want this dream and how hard you're working to get it, they will bend over backward to help you, even if it means looking at entertainment in a whole new way. You just have to be brave enough to tell them your limits and be creative enough to find ways to make it enjoyable and affordable for everyone. When you are the planner of the activity, this makes the job a lot easier.

This is perhaps the toughest part of the budgeting process, when you find out that some of the people close to you hang by such a tenuous thread, that the idea of not being able to eat out together can end your friendship. It's also the time you find out who your allies are, develop deeper relationships with people who have a similar mindset about life, and gain the support you need to reach your goal.

These are the same people who will cheer you on when you start living the big dream you're saving for now.

Holding Your Ground

Not every friendship will fall on the two extremes of these personal stories. In fact, most will fall squarely in the middle. But you need to recognize both extremes before they happen so you can be prepared to "bless and release" the ones that aren't supportive and embrace the fledgling relationships that can be your lifeline now and in the future.

No one was jealous of our lifestyle at first. Not one bit. We took public transportation when they drove, complimented them on their new clothes while they continued to see us in the same things over and over again, and listened patiently to their stories of travel – cruises, mountain getaways, and island retreats – as we stayed put.

We continued to use our Phrase to Save: "Do we want X more than we want the trip?" It was a good reminder of why we were living lean and that our gratification was just slightly delayed.

People often questioned us about what we were doing (because of what we obviously weren't doing), and it often felt like being an exhibit. Even at the start of this endeavor, we were setting ourselves apart from everyone else by the things we chose not to do as much as the things we did.

Fast forward to the present and we are traveling around the world, still on exhibit, but with a much different kind of attention. People want to know how we did it – the same kind of people, I might add, who questioned our extreme savings plan in the beginning.

> ### *People will think you're weird. Get used to it.*

Your saving grace in all of this is that you will soon be living a different life – your dream! – and when you do, other people will be in awe of how it happened, even though they were right there all along. Your Action Plan is only weird until it produces visible results.

(The same people who thought you were weird will now become your biggest champions. Strange, huh?)

Weirdo to Winner

J.K. Rowling was a broke single parent who spent her limited spare time writing Harry Potter books in coffee shops around Edinburgh. She couldn't even afford a laptop and wrote out her stories in longhand. She was on public assistance, caring for her young daughter alone, and writing as quickly as she could so she could be finished in time to take a teacher's certificate course that would help her land a job. She was recently divorced, her beloved mother had just died, and she was broke. I'm pretty sure her friends must have thought she was nuts to focus on this little boy wizard in a fantasy world when her actual world was falling apart around her.

You probably don't have it that bad. J.K. Rowling would not have even been able to afford the moderate price of the book you're holding in your hands. If she could actively chase her dream with all those odds against her, you can definitely do it.

She is now worth an estimated $1 billion, and her characters are recognizable to people all over the world. She guided her characters through to the end of the most successful book series ever written and saw them made into popular films. She believed in herself, kept going when everything around her said to give up, and now she is celebrated for her tenacity and determination.

What do you think of those people who knew her way back when, the ones who doubted her sanity when she persisted in writing every single day with no book contract, no guarantee of publication, and no prospects for any kind of success on the horizon? Do they think she's crazy now, or do they brag that they knew her back in her salad days? You know the answer to that one.

Too often people judge the success or failure of an endeavor by the process it takes to get there.

If it is too hard, or takes too long, or requires too much attention, they ridicule it. But after the endeavor succeeds, they forget the sacrifice and commitment they poo-pooed and just marvel at the achievement. Your endeavor will be the same way, and you need to keep this in mind when your inner voices – and the outer critics in your life – speak up.

We don't have the same kind of celebrity or money as J.K. Rowling, but we do know what it's like to go from being part of the crowd to standing off to the side.

That's the thing with life changes, though. Your choices will always be odd to some people, just as their choices might be odd to you.

Being different is good. Consider it a public service to give other people something to talk about.

Asking for Help

You know what's not too hard? Getting help when you're obviously in need. People rally with food, money, time and resources when you are sick, in a bind, going through a divorce or job layoff, or with the joyful stress of bringing a new child home or moving to a new house.

It isn't too tough to ask for or receive help during those times (even if you have to offer free pizza and beer to get help with a move), so we're not going to talk about that next. Instead, we're focusing on requesting help when things are going pretty well and the help you need is going to take your life from good to better. You know what I mean here: getting feedback on a good idea to improve it, introductions to speed the path to a new job / date / friendship, or support and accountability in a new physical fitness program. For whatever reason, you feel guilty asking for help when you are not in obvious 'need.' Never is this truer than when going after your dreams. You don't want to put anybody out, and you feel self-centered for asking. But people generally do want to help – including you – so it is puzzling why we are so reluctant to ask.

This is such a big disconnect that cognitive neuroscientists, psychologists and economists – an unlikely trio – have teamed up to study[2] why people choose to help. University of Arizona psychology researcher Luke Chang says:

> *"One idea is that most people cooperate because it feels good to do it. And there is some brain imaging data that shows activity in reward-related regions of the brain when*

*people are cooperating. But there is a whole
other world of motivation to do good because
you don't want to feel bad. That is the idea
behind guilt aversion."*

Whether your friends and colleagues are into feeling good or avoiding feeling bad, you can now ignore your feelings of guilt for asking for help unless your friends are sociopaths – in which case, you need new friends.

How to Ask for Help When Times Are Good

The worst-case scenario when asking for help is you get a "no," and that's no worse than the automatic no you get from not asking. Since we've learned your non-sociopathic friends want to help you out of the desire for good feelings or the avoidance of bad feelings and that the worst you can expect is a no, let's get to the business of how to ask for help when times are good.

Share your excitement/opportunity

If you aren't excited about it, people won't be very excited to help. This is why having a name for your dream and a plan to make it happen will be so appealing to other people. Work out how you will showcase your opportunity – sell it, baby, sell it! – so others can catch your enthusiasm. You don't start a movement with a whisper, sell a book without promotion, or get elected without a campaign.

Start talking about your project or idea long before you need help so people will already be familiar with what you are doing. Brenda did this in sharing the news gently but regularly with her father.

Be specific in your request

No one has given your idea as much thought as you have, so you can't expect them to intuitively know that you need help or how they can best assist you. Be very specific in what you need, and ask people according to the level of relationship you already have with them and their own interests, abilities, and time constraints.

When we started cutting back on our entertainment spending, we still wanted to spend time with our friends. Instead of keeping it to ourselves to figure out, we simply told them we needed cheaper options for dates. We gave them specific dollar amounts we were willing to spend for a happy hour, dinner, or outing, and they became pros at scouting great deals we could all enjoy. They wanted to help us save and still have fun, and it was an easy thing for them to do. It also saved us from the temptation of those more expensive nights out just to see our friends.

Pinpoint your need so the other person knows exactly what is desired of them.

Make it easy for people to help you

When you ask for help, make sure you have done as much of the legwork as you can. We did a lot of research during our 2 years of saving on everything related to long-term travel. When we had a question we couldn't get an answer to anywhere else, we asked some of the people we found online who were doing it. We didn't waste their time by asking a general question like, "how did you do it?" We asked very specific questions about gear and travel and made it as easy as possible for them to help us. When people know you're doing your homework, they are happy to help on the details. But people resent being asked for a lot of help from someone who is not doing anything to help themselves.

Go the extra mile and make it easy (and fun, if possible) for people to help you.

Thank them

Please and thank you are always welcome. Do not take for granted anyone's help, even if you don't think it took much for them to do it. No one forgets your appreciation – or your lack of it. More than that, people like to know how they were able to help you, so if you can circle back and tell them, do it. Let them know how their advice or deed helped you get closer to your dream. Thank them for making it possible, even if it only took them a second to do it.

Thank your contributors and let them know how their help contributed to your success.

Return the favor

Most of your friends won't be keeping tabs on this, but you should always be willing to help out where you can. Not everyone is good at asking for help, so check in on a regular basis and offer your expertise. Stay in touch with your friends and acquaintances so you know what they have going on in their lives. When you consistently look to add value to the lives of your friends, they will naturally want to do the same for you. We cooperate because it makes us feel good. Zig Ziglar famously said, "If you help enough people get what they want, you'll get what you want, too."

Another option for returning the favor is using the good old-fashioned barter system. You can often trade your skills and talents for those of other people, so the payback happens at the same time you are getting help. When we were working on this book, we did some business and website consulting for a few people in exchange for their help in researching media outlets and providing critical feedback. You may not always have something to barter, but when you can this is a very effective strategy for getting help. Don't be afraid to suggest this.

Offer your help in return, either right then with a barter or by checking in regularly afterward. Do not forget your karmic obligations.

Chapter Summary

As much hard work as you put in toward your dream, it won't make it to the finish line without the help of other people. You'll want and need their support, ideas, and cooperation to bring your dream to life. One way to do this is share your dream with enthusiasm, giving your top-tier friends first crack at supporting your new goal so that others will quickly follow.

Most people will be supportive, but you may get some backlash. The key is not taking it personally and remembering all feedback is based on the person giving it, not the person receiving it. You are being judged by their own aspirations and insecurities, and you should weigh the feedback accordingly.

When you practice giving in your everyday life you will feel far less guilt when asking for help in reaching your dream. You will come to appreciate the circular nature of life and how we all need to give and receive help as part of our life's journey. The more you focus on living your life this way, the easier it will be for you to ask for help when you need it.

In the next chapter we'll talk about the psychological benefits of taking action toward your dream and how this will impact your personality and behavior. You're about to get smarter and wiser!

Chapter 16: Enrich Your Life

"Everyone thinks of changing the world, but no one thinks of changing himself."

~Leo Tolstoy

There are benefits far beyond the bank account when it comes to chasing your dream. We found these out quite by accident, and we love how this one activity made such an impact on us in so many ways. As you work the Action Plan to your dream, you'll pick up a few other perks, too. Consider them bonuses.

Increased Creativity

You will learn to throw parties on a budget, scour the city for fun and inexpensive things to do, and do things for yourself that you previously hired out (hair color, anyone?). You will stop thinking "I can't afford that" and start thinking, "how can I make that happen?"

> *This is a huge mental shift that will serve you in more ways than just financially.*

Even now, this can-do attitude impacts our lives as we travel the world and write books. Activities we would have never considered before are now regular events, and we've learned how to think creatively. A budget is limiting only in your spending. Your imagination has no limits.

Take my 39th birthday, for instance. I was starting to feel the pinch. Not only was I one year closer to 40, but I also had only six months left to get rid of the rest of my possessions and say goodbye to our fantastic life and friends in Seattle.

Birthdays are a big deal for me, and I typically celebrate mine all month long by getting together with friends for parties, lunch dates, and coffee. It doesn't hurt that my birthday is in December, a banner month for parties everywhere. It's almost like an early New Year celebration for me, and I want to touch base with all my "people" to get it started off right.

This year was going to be different because I was starting the process of saying goodbye to all of them. Not only was I giving up my lifestyle and all my possessions, I was given up the daily interactions with my close group of friends, and it wasn't until the approach of my last birthday in Seattle that I fully realized it.

I tried to think of a way to make my last birthday in Seattle memorable, both for me and for my friends. And I certainly didn't want them to buy me anything when I still had a house full of stuff to go through.

That's when I came upon the idea of **a Reverse Birthday Party**. I pulled out 39 of my favorite things – like a silk scarf from France, my favorite red beret from Boston, a buttery leather coat I bought right after my divorce – and put together a little consignment shop in the living room.

I spent hours creating "sales tags" that detailed the history behind each item, where I bought it, why I loved it so much, and when I most liked to wear it. Because all of my Seattle friendships were four years old or less, it was a great way to share some of my earlier history with them and encourage them to share more about their lives before meeting me. It also helped me appreciate the history of my belongings one last time before letting them go.

My friends were instructed not to buy gifts but to plan on "shopping" at my Reverse Birthday Boutique. They each arrived with a wine bottle or snack in hand to add to the overflowing table of food I had prepared that day, and one special friend showed up with my favorite birthday cake – the one only my mom makes – and made me cry all over the toasted coconut. The evening was full of those kind of magical, teary, happy moments, and I can't see coconut now without thinking of my fabulous friend Pat – who hates coconut, by the way – and how he spent the afternoon creating this special cake for me.

There was a fantastic energy in the air as my friends came in, poured a glass of wine, and began scouring for treasures together. They held up items for opinions from the crowd, suggested items to each other, and gave thumbs up and thumbs down just like they would on any shopping trip together.

When they read something on the tag that intrigued them, they would stop to ask me about it or tell me of a similar or totally dissimilar experience. It was a fabulous way to bond with these women I love, and it gave us all a bit better insight into each other.

As they found items they liked, they wrote their names on the back of the tags. If a tag only had one name, the person who claimed it could keep it. Simple enough. If a tag had more than one name, however, we had to invoke the "Style Off" rule. Each person on the tag had to walk the runway wearing the item and we voted on who wore it best.

You can imagine with a group of fabulous women, a bit of wine, and the soundtrack of Carly Simon's "*You're*

So Vain" that this quickly became the highlight of the evening.

It was a night of love and laughter and plenty of wine and food. My friends took away almost all the items that night, I was able to share a beautiful moment with people who love me, and instead of more possessions I had a little bit of cash to add to the trip fun.

The best part? My friend Karen took a picture of me with each person and the item(s) they bought so I still have a memory of both the item and the person who bought it.

It was just about the easiest way to get rid of dear items that I could imagine. What surprised me most about the evening was the ease at which I could let things go when I knew they were going to be with the people I loved. In fact, I was amazed at how well "my" things looked on everyone else!

That gorgeous cocktail ring that I loved but always thought looked a little showy looked fabulous on my tall, regal friend. And the red beret fit my other friend's cute, heart-shaped face much better than it ever did mine. The buttery smooth leather jacket fit my slimmer friend like a glove and she didn't have any divorce memories to mar the feeling of wearing it.

Creativity is the mother of invention, and I can say without a doubt that this was the best birthday party of my life.

Better Health

Because transportation and entertainment costs are typically high, you will find yourself walking a lot more while on a budget. You may be walking around the block for entertainment and conversation after dinner each night, or exploring the trails in your area on the weekend as a low-cost activity. You may even walk more after parking in a central location to avoid additional parking fees.

Whatever the reason, you will find yourself using your feet a lot more than you used to. The benefit to this is a bit of weight loss combined with better cardiovascular health. You will also find it a great environment for chats with your partner, your friends, or even visiting with neighbors you rarely see. Being outside the distractions of work, home, car, and the phone can provide a perfect environment for connecting more deeply with other people or just clearing your mind to think about things that are important to you.

When we stopped eating out we also began consuming healthier foods, bypassing convenience items and fast food for real fruits and vegetables and home-cooked meals. We never knew food could taste so good or that we would enjoy the ritual of preparing food together each evening. It's a great time to catch up with each other and transition from work to home.

Your budget will have you rethinking many things, but the most powerful thing we did was lace up our shoes and take to the street. It served us well before we left on our big adventure, and it laid the groundwork for the hiking and trekking we came to love on our travels. I'm not sure we would have been so keen to try those things if we hadn't walked all over Seattle in the two years before we left on the journey.

We've continued with walking as our main form of exercise and transportation and have lost a combined total of 85 pounds (39 kg). We've also normalized our cholesterol and blood pressure readings and reduced the levels of inflammation in our bodies. I don't think we would have ever started walking if it weren't for the money savings, and in return it has added years of life expectancy and mobility.

Appreciating the Value – and the Cost

You will learn to assess the value of everything – what it costs you in more than just money and whether it is worth having. It will become second nature, and you will be surprised at how often you truly want to say no to something when many people just accept what is offered without evaluating the true cost. You will be more discerning about what comes into your life and therefore what comes out of your life.

I was walking through downtown Seattle with a friend one afternoon when we passed by someone handing out fliers for a local restaurant. She took the one handed to her, while I held up my hand and said "No, thank you."

We kept walking.

We were going to a charity event that afternoon, and as we found the door and registration table, we were handed goodie bags full of items. I quickly scanned the contents of mine, took the one thing I would definitely use – the lip balm – and asked my friend if she wanted my bag. She grabbed it up right away – before I changed my mind – and then asked why I wasn't keeping it.

It was full of coupons and samples for products I would never buy, and I knew if I brought it home it would clutter my life. It just wouldn't fit. I don't use those types of products, and coupons to places outside my budget would only make me think of what I could be missing.

As we've said before, advertising is more powerful than you can imagine.

So I choose not to take these "free" things into my life, because they always have a cost.

I told her my reasoning, and reminded her of the flier she got on our way over. She said she had never actually thought of saying no when something free was offered to her, whether she needed it or not. Neither did I for a long time.

Once you start putting a red velvet rope around your life, you'll spend far less money on crap, wade through less trash in your personal life, and be able to focus on the really great things that add to your happiness.

Standing up to Scrutiny

People notice what is different from them. When you dye your hair blond, get a tattoo, or wear a cowboy hat in the city you will get attention. You can also stop spending and see how many people take notice. Some will think it an oddity, and some will consider it a challenge to their own spending habits. Either way, you're setting yourself apart and opening yourself up to scrutiny.

Once you do this for a short period of time you'll become comfortable with it, mastering a skill that will help you tremendously throughout your life. I'm betting that dream you're saving for is probably a little bit "out there" for most of your friends and family, so getting used to the attention over the savings plan is going to give you a head start in standing up to the scrutiny of when you start actually living your dream.

Call it a dress rehearsal.

Even though we had downsized to one car, we tried to see if we could live without one entirely. It sat in our garage while we took buses, shuttles, and used a car-share service to test the feasibility of living without a car.

Because we lived in a city with a nearby grocery store, post office, movie rental store, and tons of restaurants, we did not anticipate a big problem. Warren even signed up to take the free shuttle to work every day at 6 am, which eliminated his commuting costs and the aggravation that went along with it.

At the time I was consulting with small business owners, so most of my work was done via phone and Internet with occasional in-person meetings. But a lot of my networking and marketing was done face-to-face, and one of the biggest meetings I attended each month was located in Bellevue, a suburb of Seattle.

Like most US suburbs, Bellevue is a little swankier than the city it borders and there is less walking and more driving. Houses are bigger, there are many more malls and shopping centers, and people maintain a greater personal space around themselves than they do in the city.

The first time I took the bus from my neighborhood to the meeting in Bellevue, it took an hour. (When I drove, it took 45 minutes.) I was let off less than a block from the meeting space, and I arrived without anyone knowing how I got there.

We did the usual meet and greet before the luncheon started, and then we all took our seats at tables for 8. Part of the ritual was to say something interesting about yourself and your business, so I mentioned that I was experimenting with living without a car and how that related to my usual business advice of questioning every expense and activity as a solo entrepreneur so that your efforts and money are always being spent on the core of your business first.

One woman at the table literally had her jaw drop when I told her I had taken the bus from Seattle to Bellevue. I can assure you that I was the only woman out of 150 who had done so. The other women at the table were less than impressed, and I was sure as we went around the table that I had lost their attention – and a great marketing opportunity for my business – by talking about our little life experiments.

Later the woman found me and questioned me about my motives and I told her the how and why of it. As a woman who had never taken public transportation in her life, she was fascinated that I would choose to do it when I had a car in the garage.

Because I was unafraid to advertise what I was doing, I drew the attention of a woman who was also working on big changes in her life, though in a different way. I would have never known that upon meeting her, and it was only because I had 'outed' my experiment that she chose to begin sharing some of hers.

We became fast friends – friends to this day, in fact – and if I hadn't mentioned my bus experiment I doubt I would have registered on her radar among all those other people.

Bonus points: She also became a client.

And she still hasn't taken public transportation.

Reaching Your Goal

So, what happens when you follow your Action Plan for your Dream? Well, strangely enough, you actually do reach it.

(Funny how that happens!)

When you reach your savings target and cross off the date you set on the calendar, your next job is to take that cash out of The Vault and start living your dream. This is the portion of the book you start writing yourself, because everyone's dream is different.

Beth became a published author and has been working full-time in her business since 2012. She cherishes the time she can spend with her son and the freedom and creativity she gets from her work. She is enjoying the success of her book, which is now also being sold in multiple foreign markets.

Akiyo is sharing her lifestyle success with other sufferers of bipolar disorder and Asperger's Syndrome. She is writing a book in her adopted new home of Edinburgh, Scotland, where she and her boyfriend still live the minimalist's life in just one room of their apartment. They are now saving up to go travelling for a year in 3 years' time – just in time for her next super-manic phase. She is sewing, taking trapeze lessons, and making jewelry when she isn't traveling or working.

Matt and his family are on sabbatical in Indonesia at the time of this writing. We just learned they are making the move permanent after a side business they started blossomed. They expect to be living there full-time in just 6 months.

Samantha continues to create fun and beautiful cakes for all the birthdays, special events, and weddings in her area. She even created the cake for our last book launch, exposing her skills to an international audience.

Brenda continues to teach English in Brazil and enjoys a more laid-back lifestyle. She's considering a move to Asia to explore more of the world as an English teacher.

An Action Plan for Dreamers

When we started with our Dream in 2008 we felt a little bit crazy even considering it. But we moved forward with our plan anyway.

1. We took our fuzzy notion and **Discovered our Dream**.

2. Then we started planning it out, visualizing what it would look like, and **Making it Real.**

3. We made sure we were **Aligned with Each Other** so we'd be a stronger team.

4. We bought a snazzy piece of **Dream Porn** in the form of a giant world map so we could continue dreaming with direction. We gave our dream a name.

5. Then we **Put a Number to our Dream**.

6. We used that figure to **Set the Date** for our dream.

7. After that, we set up **The Vault** to house our dream money.

8. We **Calculated our Current Spending** and determined our financial status.

9. We had already **Eliminated our Credit Card Debt**, but we made sure to continue paying off the balance each month.

10. We created a **Phrase to Save** to help us stay on track: "Do we want this more than we want our dream life?"

11. We **Analyzed and Cut Expenses** to make room for our dream to grow.

12. We **Created a Roadmap** with our new spending and saving goals and stuck to it.

13. We **Created Additional Income** through side jobs and selling our junk.

14. We performed a **Monthly Financial Review** to adjust our goals and stay on track.

15. We learned to how to get **Social Support** and manage **Peer Pressure**. We realized we don't need permission to take action toward our dream.

16. We absorbed the **Life Lessons** from the process and continue using them as our dream grows and evolves.

We learned that standing out from the crowd gave us a better view anyway. Mostly we learned about focus, determination, and action. But we had to, you see. We decided early on to make the trip longer, to really savor traveling around the world even if we did it on a budget. The excitement of living our dream was just so overwhelming we knew we couldn't stop at one year. Because of that, when we finally left on October 1, 2010, we had enough money in The Vault to travel the world for five years.

Five Years.

You may recall when this whole thing started we were planning for one year of travel. I can't really blame us for aiming low – we just didn't know how much we'd love it or how good we'd be at saving and making money. But after going through this experience we can only conclude that putting a laser-like focus on financing your dream will reap rewards bigger than you can even imagine.

It's not just the money

Our neighbors donated the unlimited use of their gorgeous mountain home in Ecuador, and this is where we spent the first seven weeks of our trip, learning Spanish and acclimating to a new altitude and a new way of life. The funniest part? We had lived next door to them for two years and never even knew they had a vacation home, much less one in Ecuador. They were some of the biggest supporters in our dream, and it all started by telling them about it one day at the mailbox.

As we got closer to our departure date, friends and friends of friends began making connections for us in countries all around the world. We had places to stay in Colombia and Argentina and the UK and India and more...it just boggles the mind that these strangers would open their homes to us or show us around their cities.

When we sold our home in May, we had to find a furnished place to live until our departure on October 1, one that was nearby so Warren could continue to use the work shuttle service. Our good friend offered us a great room at her beautiful home a mile away, and we paid the same amount we would have paid for a basic furnished apartment. We joked that by downsizing we had landed in the lap of luxury. It was wonderful to spend our last few months with a great friend.

Our friends hosted several backyard BBQs the summer before we left, and we were able to see all of them at a very low cost. We had two going away parties, one for all our friends and the other a more intimate dinner with our closest friends the night before we left. We said the kind of things you should say to the people you love but never do, and we're so glad that we had the opportunity to do so.

And now?

Well, now we just call this a lifestyle. We've been continually traveling and living as temporary residents in countries all over the world since 2010, and we have no plans to stop. We continue to use the budget lessons we learned from our Action Plan to live a fuller, more focused life than the one we lived before for less money. We challenge ourselves on a regular basis, and our dream continues to evolve. We have already achieved it once, so we know we can achieve it again. In fact, in 2012 we took a 6-month overland journey (no planes allowed) from Thailand all the way across Asia and Europe. It was a challenging and rewarding 6-month adventure; one I don't think we would have been able to do just a few short years ago. You know, back before we had the confidence achieving this dream gave us.

We have very few worries, no alarm clocks, and no bills. Our life is richer than we could have ever imagined.

All this is waiting for you, too. As we said at the beginning, you are already halfway to changing your habits just by buying this book. Don't just be inspired by our story; take action.

Flip back to Chapter 1 and start thinking specifically as to how you want your life to change. Write out the dream you have in mind, and for heaven's sake make yourself some juicy Dream Porn. Give your dream a worthy name, one that makes you smile every time you say it. Put a price on your vision and then set the deadline for making it real. Find a Vault to store your cash, and figure out where your money is going now. Get rid of your credit card debt, because no dream needs it. Create your Phrase to Save so you'll be strong when temptation strikes. Cut your expenses in favor of your dream. Refine your Roadmap so it will take you in a straight line to your dream. Earn some extra cash through a side hustle or sell some of the possessions you won't need in your new life. Stay on track with a Monthly Financial Review. Gain the support of your friends, ask for help when you need it, and learn to withstand peer pressure. Absorb the lessons from this whole glorious process and get thee to living the dream, friend.

Once you complete your Action Plan and achieve your dream, nothing will ever be out of your reach again. You'll be disciplined, creative, and confident in your ability to reach your goals, and life will be an ever-evolving series of challenges and wins as you think better, dream bigger, and learn that money is a means to an end, not the end itself.

You've seen what can happen with our story. It all starts with taking the first step, and you've already done that by reading this book. Just put one foot in front of the other and keep going until you reach your dream. Now flip back to page 1 and get to work.

Your dream is waiting to become a reality.

Acknowledgements

This book would not have been possible without the support of our readers who travel virtually with us every day at www.MarriedwithLuggage.com. Special thanks go to those readers who went above and beyond the call of duty by reading early drafts of the first edition and providing invaluable feedback: Akiyo Kano, PhD; Tranque Fuller; Rob Philip; Paz Chentnik; and Amber Singleton Riviere. You guys are terrific, and we love that you're as passionate about chasing your dreams as we are.

Our second edition was greatly helped by the fabulous Guy Kawasaki, who showed us a few new tricks in self-publishing with his book, APE. Akiyo Kano, PhD again provided line-by-line feedback, and Vi Proskurovska, Michelle Oakes, Samantha Searle, Matt Koenig, and Beth Hayden made insightful observations that greatly improved this book.

Special thanks to our friends who went above and beyond the call of duty in helping us finish this book. Alison Cornford-Matheson and Andrew Matheson let us take over their dining room table for over a week to finish the first edition in Brussels. They kept us fed and even made us leave to have fun a few times. Alison also took the great author photos.

Our gratitude goes to designer Shea McGuier for taking this project to another level with her cover design, layout, and website graphics. You made us look professional long before we completed the project, and your good nature, attention to detail and enthusiasm made the final product even better than we could have hoped.

We could not forget to thank Angela Barton, who edited the first edition for content and flow as well as performed a full line-by-line edit to correct our grammar to help our ideas shine through. You gave us bad news with a soft touch and cheered the good news with a megaphone. You really kept us going at the end, and we are forever grateful for your support. It was a real pleasure to finally meet you in person prior to publication of this second edition. You are just as great in real life as you've been virtually all these years.

Finally, we'd like to thank the readers who have shared their experiences with us publicly via comments, privately through email, in person over coffee or beer, and even through Skype. We've loved getting to know you and are honored you would share your challenges and successes with us. You inspire us to keep living our dream.

About the Authors

Warren and Betsy Talbot gave up successful careers and a cozy life in Seattle to travel the world. They spent two years planning, downsizing, and saving for the adventure of a lifetime. They left in time to celebrate their 40th birthdays on the road, and they are more convinced than ever that this was the right decision. A dream you can touch and feel is exponentially better than the one hundred that stay locked in your head and heart.

They finished writing this second edition in the beautiful city of Guanajuato, Mexico.

Stay in touch with Betsy and Warren:

Twitter: @betsytalbot and @warrentalbot

Facebook: www.Facebook.com/MarriedwithLuggage

Email: info@marriedwithluggage.com

Website: www.MarriedwithLuggage.com

Flickr: www.Flickr.com/photos/marriedwithluggage

Action Plan for Dreamers

1. Discover Your Dream

2. Make it So Real You Can Touch it

3. Align Your Desires With Your Partner

4. Create Dream Porn and Give Your Dream a Name

5. Price Your Dream

6. Set the Date

7. Secure Your Vault

8. Calculate Your Spending

9. Address Credit Card Debt

10. Create Your Phrase to Save

11. Cut Expenses to Make Room for Your Dream

12. Refine Your Roadmap

13. Create Additional Income

14. Perform a Monthly Financial Review

15. Enlist Support and Manage Peer Pressure

16. Absorb the Life Lessons

Resources

Savings

- Smarty Pig: www.SmartyPig.com
- Debt reduction: www.LearnVest.com
- Get Rich Slowly:
    www.GetRichSlowly.org

Budgeting

- Mint: www.Mint.com
- MoneyDashboard (UK):
    www.MoneyDashboard.com

Negotiating

- I Will Teach You to be Rich:
    www.IWillTeachYouToBeRich.com

Selling your stuff

- Selling your home: Married with Luggage blog (goo.gl/yVkTC)
- *Getting Rid of It: Eliminate the Clutter in Your Life* by Betsy and Warren Talbot:

    www.MarriedwithLuggage.com/getting-rid-of-it/

- Cancel Magazines and catalogs:
  https://www.catalogchoice.org/

Television

- Hulu.com (US)
- tvcatchup.com (UK)
- Google "watch tv free online in ____" for options in your country
- Video on living without cable:
  youtu.be/6UJUbS3_1qM

Glossary

The Vault is the account where you will keep your money. It is a one-way street. You can't touch this. In fact, imagine a very large guard dog in front of the Vault door. Money goes in, but it does not come out until you have hit your goal.

The Roadmap is your budget, the guide along this savings journey. You will start out with a crappy one, and your job is to refine it over time, making adjustments every month to move you closer to your goal. We'll show you how.

Dream Porn is your big visual, the reminder you place in a prominent space to keep your goal front and center. You will need this reminder on the days when you're weak, tired, or getting a lot of peer pressure to spend.

Phrase to Save is the mantra you will develop to keep you on track with your daily spending and celebrate your savings. We'll show you how to develop yours based on your budget numbers and your dream.

Monthly Financial Review is just that, a review of your savings and spending for the month. We have created a handy checklist for you to use each month to continue refining your Roadmap as you go along. Remember, if you're saving with a partner you need to review with a partner. The focus is always on solving problems and moving forward, not blaming or shaming.

End Notes

We have made every effort to insure these links are correct at the time of publication. However, we do not control these websites and they may move, change, or delete pages. Where possible, we have given you the website name and topic so you can easily search for the reference should the link be broken.

Chapter 1

[1] We wrote about The 5 Whys Method of Problem Solving on the Married with Luggage website:

www.marriedwithluggage.com/the-5-whys-in-problem-solving/

[2] Learn How to Get the Respect You Deserve on the Married with Luggage website:

www.marriedwithluggage.com/2012/05/17/how-to-get-the-respect-you-deserve/

[3] Find out how to Nurture the Seeds of Inspiration on the Married with Luggage website:

www.marriedwithluggage.com/2012/06/18/find-your-dream/

Dumb Little Man is a personal growth and productivity site. This article provides 22 questions and actions to help you discover your dream:

www.dumblittleman.com/2007/08/22-secrets-to-

discovering-your-dream.html

43 Things is a bucket list site. Users list all the things they want to do and check them off. Get inspired by seeing what other people are doing: www.43Things.com.

People all over the world use www.Meetup.org to find people with similar interests. Type in your city and then explore the groups open to you, often for no charge.

Learn how to make new friends based on your interests at Married with Luggage:

www.marriedwithluggage.com/2012/06/08/how-

to-make-new-friends

Dr. Arthur Agatston was the source we turned to on the advice of my preventive cardiologist. We both have a family history of heart disease, and the common-sense approach to nutrition via the South Beach Diet helped us relearn how to fortify our bodies and lower our cholesterol: www.southbeachdiet.com/diet/dr-agatston (as always, check with your physician before starting any new diet or exercise program).

Penelope Trunk writes about careers and her challenges with Asperger's Syndrome. Her posts are often blunt and controversial, but you can learn a lot from her transparent journey from city girl to farm girl:

blog.penelopetrunk.com/2011/03/07/beware-of-

leo-babautas-minimalist-lifestyle/

Chapter 2

Household saving rates: Source:

www.oecd-ilibrary.org/economics/household-saving-rates-forecasts_2074384x-table7

Harvard Womens' Health Watch on why change is hard:

www.health.harvard.edu/newsletters/Harvard_Womens_Health_Watch/2012/March/why-behavior-change-is-hard-and-why-you-should-keep-trying

YouTube video of the popular 1999 Monster.com commercial "When I grow up:"

www.youtube.com/watch?v=S7pijrAOLdg

Chapter 3

Getting to Yes by Roger Fisher and William Ury is the basis for this helpful article on principled negotiation:

www.colorado.edu/conflict/peace/treatment/pricneg.htm

Chapter 4

We made over $8000 by selling most of our possessions on Craigslist. You can learn to declutter your home and make some cash on the things that no longer fit your life by following the practical suggestions in *Getting Rid of It: Eliminate the Clutter in Your Life*. It is available at all the main online booksellers in both ebook and paperback format, and if you choose to buy it we would love it if you left a review. You can find links to buy it on our website here:

www.MarriedwithLuggage.com/getting-rid-of-it/

[2]Pinterest.com is an online bulletin board where users 'pin' photos and articles in categories. You can follow someone else's boards and allow others to follow yours. For any type of visual project, it can be addictive. You can set up your own Pinterest account for free at www.Pinterest.com/ and we hope you'll visit our boards at www.Pinterest.com/WWWBD

[3]Beth documented the naming of her dream on her website: bloggingwithbeth.com/leap/. Be sure to note the supportive comments.

[4] If you do want to take it a step further and start a blog to document your journey, by all means do. You can start one in minutes at www.Wordpress.com. We did this the day after we decided to go after our dream, and in the years since it has grown into a great little publishing company for our practical message of creating the life you want out of the life you already have. If nothing else, journaling or blogging your progress will give you a way to track your goal and work through problems along the way.

Chapter 5

[1]Find out how much we spend every month in our travels at www.RTWExpenses.com. You can also search online for "how much does it cost to X" with X being your dream or a component of your dream.

[2]Smarty Pig is an online savings account available in the US and Australia. Visit www.SmartyPig.com/

[3] Mint is an online financial dashboard for management of all your financial accounts. You can link

your accounts directly to Mint.com for easy, at-a-glance reporting of your financial situation. The service is free at www.Mint.com/. Mint is owned by Intuit and is available in the US and Canada. Mint makes money through ads and offering you financial services like credit cards through third-parties. Always read the fine print and understand the risks before divulging your account information and passwords to any service.

· MoneyDashboard is an online financial dashboard for management of all your financial accounts. . You can link your accounts directly to Mint.com for easy, at-a-glance reporting of your financial situation. The service is free and is available to citizens of the UK. Always read the fine print and understand the risks before divulging your account information and passwords to any service.

Chapter 6

¹Find out more about Beth and her book, *Pinfluence: The Complete Guide to Marketing Your Business with Pinterest,* at her website www.bethhayden.com/

² We made over $8000 by selling most of our possessions on Craigslist. You can learn to declutter your home and make some cash on the things that no longer fit your life by following the practical suggestions in *Getting Rid of It: Eliminate the Clutter in Your Life*. It is available at all the main online booksellers in both ebook and paperback format, and if you choose to buy it we would love it if you left a review. You can find links to buy it on our website here:

www.MarriedwithLuggage.com/getting-rid-of-it/

Chapter 9

[1] An easy-to-read analysis of household debt by the website Nerd Wallet, based on figures from The Federal Reserve and the US Census:

www.nerdwallet.com/blog/credit-card-

data/average-credit-card-debt-household/

[2] The National Money Education Charity breaks down consumer debt as of December 2012 with some fairly alarming statistics:

www.creditaction.org.uk/helpful-resources/debt-

statistics.html

[3] The Sydney Morning Herald profiled rising consumer debt in Australia in January 2012, reporting a total of $50 billion in credit card debt for the nation:

www.smh.com.au/money/borrowing/plastic-debt-

swells-to-record-50-billion-20120112-1px49.html

[4] *I Will Teach You to be Rich* is the name of a website and a book by Ramit Sethi. You'll find numerous resources, from scripts you can use in your calls to banks to tips on saving big money on insurance and cable. Ramit focuses on substantial immediate savings over small daily savings:

www.IWillTeachYouToBeRich.com/

Chapter 10

[1] Chip and Dan Heath are experts at personal and corporate change, and you can gain numerous insights into how to effectively motivate yourself and others in

their book *Switch: How to Change Things When Change is Hard*:

    www.heathbrothers.com/switch/

 BJ Fogg, PhD, is the Director of the Persuasive Tech Lab at Stanford University. He is also the founder of Tiny Habits, a website focused on helping you make small changes. Sign up each week to track 3 tiny changes with support from Dr. Fogg. It's free:

    www.TinyHabits.com/join

Chapter 11

 Learn more about your higher self and how resistance rears its ugly head at the moment you are closest to success in Steven J. Pressfield's excellent short book, *Do the Work*:

    www.stevenpressfield.com/do-the-work/

 Betsy wrote about demanding love and romance every day of the year, not just on a consumer holiday like Valentine's Day, on our website:

    www.marriedwithluggage.com/2010/02/12/im-

    taking-back-february-14/

 The 3-Day Novel Contest is a way for aspiring novelists to try their hand at writing a book over the US Labor Day holiday (which is sorta weird, since it is a Canadian company). It's fast and furious, and editors have been combing through these very rough drafts for 35 years to find hidden gems. One lucky author gets a book deal out of it every year. Find out more at: www.3daynovel.com

Chapter 12

Before you eliminate your telephone land line, make sure you have emergency coverage for police, fire, and ambulance via your cell phone. 911 (US & Canada), 999 (UK) , 000 (Australia), and 111 (New Zealand) may not be able to pinpoint your location with a cell phone in an emergency situation. We lived without a land line for 4 years in Seattle.

Chapter 13

Learn how to start your own $100 side business with your existing skills and talents in Chris Guillebeau's book, *The $100 Startup.* You'll find several case studies to inspire you: www.100startup.com

See how Warren advertises his website development services: www.MWLDevelopment.com

Nicole Donnelly turned baby leg warmers into a million-dollar company: www.BabyLegs.com/. (Babylegs was eventually sold for an undisclosed figure to United Legwear.)

Dany Levy was the "go-to" person in her circle for what to do and where to go in her city. She turned this into the email you now know as Daily Candy and spawned a whole new industry of daily deals (think we would have Groupon now without Daily Candy leading the way? Probably not.) www.DailyCandy.com

Robert Stephens took his one-man college computer handyman service and grew it in to the Geek Squad. If you are the one regularly helping your friends and neighbors do something, then you already have a market. You just need to formalize it and start charging.

www.GeekSquad.com

Passive Panda is the site freelancers use to make more money. The "Side Hustle" series interviews people who are making serious money with their side jobs and include tips for you to get started. Find out more at:

www.passivepanda.com/freelance/

MSN Money tax expert Jeff Schnepper shows why planning for a tax refund is a bad financial strategy:

money.msn.com/tax-planning/why-i-hate-income-

tax-refunds-schnepper.aspx

We outlined our strategy for downsizing our possessions and making thousands of dollars via Craigslist in our book, *Getting Rid of It: Eliminate the Clutter in Your Life*. Buy it in ebook or paperback on Amazon or at

www.MarriedwithLuggage.com/getting-rid-of-it/

Chapter 15

Read more about the rain shadow and how rainfall can differ so heavily in mountain rainforest area:

www.olympicrainshadow.com/

Guilt/Cooperation Linked by Neural Network: Why People Choose to Cooperate Rather than Act Selfishly:

www.sciencedaily.com/releases/2011/05/11051113

1126.htm

See the cake Samantha created for the virtual launch party of our last book here:

www.marriedwithluggage.com/2012/03/15/virtua

l-launch-party-strip-off-your-fear/

Chapter 16

Find out how we are spending our savings in our monthly expense reports at www.RTWExpenses.com. As of this writing, we spend about $25,000 per year to live the life of our dreams.

Harvard Womens' Health Watch on why change is hard:

www.health.harvard.edu/newsletters/Harvard_W

omens_Health_Watch/2012/March/why-behavior-

change-is-hard-and-why-you-should-keep-trying

Put One Foot in Front of the Other, an animated video from the classic television show, *Santa Claus is Coming to Town*: youtu.be/OORsz2d1H7s

Acknowledgements

APE: Author Publisher Entrepreneur: How to Publish a Book, by Guy Kawasaki and Shawn Welch. Excellent advice for the new or seasoned author.

Akiyo Kano, PhD writes about goal-setting for people with bipolor syndrome and Asperger's Syndrome at:

www.goalchasers.com

Vi Proskurovska is an economist and photographer in Brussels.

Samantha Searle is a cake artist who created a 3-D image of our last book for the launch. You can see more of her creations at:

www.Facebook.com/LittleAvenueCakes/

Matt Koenig realized his dream of a family sabbatical to Indonesia. You can track his experience at www.oneyearsabbatical.com/

Beth Hayden is a sought-after speaker, trainer, and social media strategist who authored *Pinfluence: The Complete Guide to Marketing Your Business with Pinterest.* Find out more about Beth at:

www.BethHayden.com/

Find Alison Cornford-Matheson's garden and travel stock photography at ACM Photography, www.acmphotography.com/, or on her excellent Belgium expat website, www.cheeseweb.eu/

Angela Barton is a writer, film editor, and book editor. You can find out more about her and her quest for living with just enough at www.angelabarton.com

Shea McGuier turned a fun photo from our adventures in Slovenia to a happy book cover we love. She created the original ebook cover and layout as well as the new second-edition cover. You can reach Shea at:

www.onabudgetdesign.com/

Turn the Page to read a preview from the Talbot's latest book, *Married with Luggage: What We Learned About Love By Traveling the World*. Discover the behind the scenes story of Warren & Betsy's adventures and what traveling together 24/7 taught them about love and each other.

Married with Luggage

What We Learned about

Love by Traveling the World

By Betsy & Warren Talbot

Contents

Authors' Note

The incredible story of love and adventure inside this book almost didn't happen. In 2006, we were ready to throw in the towel, give up on each other, and go our separate ways. The relationship was just too hard, and neither one of us was sure we wanted to put in the work to make it right – or if we even could make it right.

But we did. And what followed was nothing short of incredible.

This book is set up in three sections. First you'll find out what went wrong and how we started turning it around, giving ourselves a fighting chance to succeed.

In the second part, we'll share the funny, embarrassing, and frightening adventures of our first year of travel.

In part three, you'll discover what we call "next level stuff," the master's lessons on love and communication that can only be forged during extreme situations like erupting volcanoes and storms at sea.

This is our love story, and we reveal a lot of ourselves in these pages. You'll find out what we fight about, what we weigh (or at least what we used to), and the stupidest, wildest, and most hair-raising things we've ever done together – all in the name of love.

The story is ours, but to make it easier to read it's written in Betsy's voice.

We hope you enjoy this peek into a love story that almost didn't happen, and that it inspires a reawakening in your own relationship.

Because in the end, all we're left with is love.

Betsy and Warren Talbot

April 23, 2014

Lubrín, Spain

PART I: UNPACKING OUR EMOTIONAL BAGGAGE

1

The Worst Experiences Make the Best Stories

We woke up in the middle of the night covered in a layer of grit. I blinked my eyes a few times, trying to orient myself. Then I remembered: we were camping on the southern coast of Turkey. My next thought: "Is the air this salty near the Mediterranean Sea?" It took only a second more to realize the grit wasn't salt but sand. The tiny grains covered my face and lay in a fine coating over my sleeping bag. Dirt blew underneath the flysheet and into the mesh-covered door of our tent from the wind raging outside. I was wide-awake.

I rolled over on my left side and saw my husband Warren's profile. When he turned toward me I could almost make out the whites of his eyes in the dark.

"I think one of the ties has come loose," he said. He sat up in his sleeping bag and reached for his clothes.

"Do you need my help?" I asked, knowing the answer. It was a one-person job and safer to have the weight of a human being inside to hold the tent down in case everything came loose. Neither one of us had to say it out loud.

Warren donned his headlamp and knelt by the front door of the tent. We executed our well practiced "mosquito maneuver," a quick in and out of the tent while the person inside zips up quickly. We developed this technique in Scotland to keep the swarming biting flies called midges out. I never dreamed we'd be using it to fight blowing sand in a storm at the edge of a cliff.

Warren used a rock to hammer the stake in deeper and retie the flysheet over our tent. The wind was so strong I could barely hear him pounding the stake outside, but I could see the light from his headlamp. His light bobbed as he walked around the tent checking all the stakes and ties and placing big rocks over them. Satisfied, he called to me that he was coming back in. After a reverse mosquito maneuver to re-enter the tent, he gave me the rundown on the situation outside.

The wind was strong, and we had little protection from it in our current location. With the tent cinched down as tight as it could be, we had to hope it was enough. We lay back down and listened to the storm outside, wondering if we'd get any more sleep that night.

Our little analog travel clock sat in a mesh pocket on the inside of the tent. We'd purchased it on our honeymoon in Paris back in 2004. I remembered the rainy day we bought it, after a lazy afternoon of wine, cheese, and sex. We needed to get up early the next morning to catch a flight home, and the room in our quaint hotel didn't have an alarm clock. I flashed back to the feeling of those soft sheets on my skin, the sweet exhaustion of new love, and the comfort of that hotel bed. The grit in my sleeping bag ended the memory and brought me back to the harsh reality of the present. We were a long way from romance in that moment.

The glowing arms of the clock showed the time as 12:10 a.m., still a long way from sunrise. Neither of us expected to get any sleep, but fatigue won and we dozed off. The time was 1:30 a.m. when we woke up again, this time to the sound of rain pelting the tent. The storm was growing.

I pulled in our bags of food and hiking boots from the outer vestibule of the tent, further crowding our small space. My go-to move when I'm nervous is to nest, to pack myself in with my necessities as I face a problem. As I rearranged our space, we evaluated our situation. Our tent was perched on a cliff jutting out toward the Mediterranean Sea on the coast of Turkey. The wind was so strong it could blow our tent out to sea if we tried to take it down. The nearest shelter was in the village we passed late the day before, at least a mile away uphill and over rocky terrain. The rocks on the cliffside trail were already slick from rain and would be dangerous to walk in the moonless and stormy night. Even if we did make it to the village, we didn't speak more than a few words of Turkish. How would the residents react to our late-night request for help? Perhaps the most distressing bit of news: no one knew where we were, and we didn't have a phone. We had no way to reach the outside world thanks to our desire for an "off the grid" experience.

The night hadn't started that way. We arrived at our scenic camp spot shortly before sunset after a full day of walking along Turkey's famed Lycian Way. Fellow walkers touted this route to us as one of the most beautiful in the world, and it was living up to the hype. The azure blue of the Mediterranean Sea sparkled as we hiked along the rugged cliffs, enjoying the occasional respite from the heat in the pine forest areas. The packs we carried were 30 pounds each, loaded down with a tent and gear to go the full distance of 300 miles over the next few weeks. We'd planned this trip for months, and it was turning out even better than we hoped.

Earlier that afternoon we enjoyed a meal with two university students we met while walking. These first-time backpackers from the bustling city of Ankara chose to rent a room at a pension for the night. Warren teased them for carrying tents they didn't plan to ever use during their weeklong hike.

After goodbyes all around, we walked down the hill toward the sea, looking for a flat area to camp. As we rounded one of the hairpin turns on the rocky trail, we spotted a flat circular area surrounded by rocks overlooking the sea. It was beautiful. Our perfect little spot was just big enough for a tent and gave us a front-row seat to the setting sun over the Mediterranean.

It didn't take us long to set up our tent, change out of our sweaty walking clothes, and ease our feet out of our boots and into our flip-flops. We high-fived each other for scoring such a great location, feeling a little bit sorry for the university students we left in the pension. Were they going to see a magnificent sunset over the Mediterranean? No way. And they were paying for a night in a cramped room while we were sitting in the lap of Mother Nature for free. *Suckers.*

We perched ourselves on a boulder with our legs swinging off the side of the cliff, eating our bread, cheese, and olives for dinner. Our night's lodging was the best we'd ever had, anywhere in the world, and we knew it. As the sun set, we talked about our hike, our life, and the grand adventures we'd have before it was over. Little did we know the adventure would escalate that night.

At 1:30 in the morning, we began discussing our situation, neither one wanting to express just how scared we were. It was like two strangers making small talk about the weather in an elevator. *Can you believe this storm? Yeah, crazy isn't it?*

"I think we should pack up our bags now on the off chance the storm gets worse and we need to leave in a hurry," I said. Part of me wanted to hear Warren call me a worrywart and reassure me that I was overreacting as usual. Instead he agreed, reaching down to the foot of his sleeping bag to get his backpack. We took turns packing, since the tight confines of the tent didn't allow us enough elbow room to do it at the same time. While focusing on the task at hand, we spoke quietly, as if there was someone sleeping next door. I'm not sure why.

"We should sleep in our clothes, just in case we need to get up in a hurry," Warren said. We changed into what we planned to wear the next day and placed our rain jackets on top of our backpacks at the foot of our sleeping bags. The walls of the tent bowed in from the wind and the rain was pouring down, but we were optimistic that we'd ride out the storm. Against all odds, we fell asleep again.

At 3:20 a.m., I woke to a gentle caress on my cheek. I opened my eyes to discover the wall of the tent pushing down on my face. The wind was raging, and the aluminum poles in our tent bent at an unnatural angle. The rain pelted our tent so hard I thought it was going to break through the fabric. Lightning flashed over the sea, casting an eerie light in the tent every few seconds. The face we each saw in that greenish light was scared to death. It was well past time to pack up and get the hell out. But where? And how?

The storm in 2013 was a perfect parallel to where our marriage was just eight years before. Back then we couldn't even navigate our way through a regular weekday in the US together, much less a violent storm on the edge of a cliff in Turkey. Our relationship was on the brink of breakup. At first we tried to ignore the dark clouds gathering over our relationship. But over time the storm grew too large to ignore, just like this storm in

Turkey. We could either find a way to safety together or let the storm destroy the relationship we built.

We chose safety.

We chose togetherness.

We chose to make our marriage work, and this is the story of how we did it.

Purchase the full edition of *Married with Luggage* to see how the story unfolds and read about our journey back from the edge. You can purchase your copy in print or eBook format from Amazon, iTunes, Barnes & Noble, and Kobo. As one reader described it: "*An uplifting and romantic story about the evolution of a marriage and the road to finding a happy balance. A true testimony to being in love.*" ~ New York Times bestselling author, Melissa Foster

Made in the USA
San Bernardino, CA
03 May 2018